The Savvy Crafter's
GUIDE TO SUCCESS

Turn Your Crafts into a Career

Sandra McCall

NORTH LIGHT BOOKS
Cincinnati, OH
www.mycraftivity.com

12 11 10 09 08   5 4 3 2 1

Distributed in Canada by Fraser Direct
100 Armstrong Avenue
Georgetown, ON, Canada L7G 5S4
Tel: (905) 877-4411

Distributed in the U.K. and Europe by David & Charles
Brunel House, Newton Abbot, Devon, TQ12 4PU, England
Tel: (+44) 1626 323200, Fax: (+44) 1626 323319
E-mail: postmaster@davidandcharles.co.uk

Distributed in Australia by Capricorn Link
P.O. Box 704, S. Windsor, NSW 2756 Australia
Tel: (02) 4577-3555

Library of Congress Cataloging-in-Publication Data

McCall, Sandra, 1953-
  Savvy crafter's guide to success / by Sandra McCall. -- 1st ed.
     p. cm.
  Includes bibliographical references and index.
  ISBN 978-1-58180-942-8 (pbk. : alk. paper)
  1. Selling--Handicraft--Handbooks, manuals, etc. 2.
Handicraft--Marketing--Handbooks, manuals, etc. I. Title.
  HF5439.H27M33 2007
  745.5068'8--dc22

2007025244

F+W PUBLICATIONS, INC.
www.fwpublications.com

Editor: Robin M. Hampton
Cover Design: Marissa Bowers
Interior Design: Marc Whitaker for MTWdesign
Production Coordinator: Greg Nock

Metric Conversion Chart

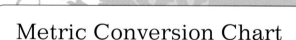

to convert	to	multiply by
Inches	Centimeters	2.54
Centimeters	Inches	0.4
Feet	Centimeters	30.5
Centimeters	Feet	0.03
Yards	Meters	0.9
Meters	Yards	1.1
Sq. Inches	Sq. Centimeters	6.45
Sq. Centimeters	Sq. Inches	0.16
Sq. Feet	Sq. Meters	0.09
Sq. Meters	Sq. Feet	10.8
Sq. Yards	Sq. Meters	0.8
Sq. Meters	Sq. Yards	1.2
Pounds	Kilograms	0.45
Kilograms	Pounds	2.2
Ounces	Grams	28.3
Grams	Ounces	0.035

Acknowledgments

To my family and to everyone who contributed so generously to this book, I thank and appreciate you with all my heart. You're all such wonderfully talented and generous souls.

About the author

Sandra McCall calls herself "a rubber-stamp and multi-medium expert." She makes art—from designing craft projects to writing articles for rubber-stamp/paper-arts books and magazines. She also designs rubber stamps for JudiKins and Stamp Oasis.

Sandra teaches art workshops across the United States. She's currently interested in resin casting, any type of fiber arts, beading on jewelry and fabric, soft block carving, polymer clay, making dolls and art figures of all kinds and painting canvases with acrylic paint.

Sandra has had several articles and artwork featured in major publications and made one DVD with PageSage called *Fabricadabra: Material Magic with Sandra McCall*. She's written four additional North Light titles: *Making Gifts with Rubber Stamps*, *30-Minute Rubber Stamp Workshop*, *Sandra McCall's Rubber Stamped Jewelry* and *Stamping Effects in Polymer Clay with Sandra McCall*.

Sandra lives in Arizona with her husband and best friend, fellow artist, Les Gains.

Contents

Journal Cover
by Sandra McCall
PHOTO BY SANDRA McCALL

Introduction

From the first inkling of the idea, I knew I wanted to be the best art/craft teacher ever. So I looked and looked for books on the finer points of teaching craft classes. Well, fifteen years ago, there wasn't a whole heck of a lot, so I had to take a big gulp and "jump in, building my wings on the way down," as the saying goes.

Since then, I've learned a lot about the subject. My students and customers enjoy grilling me on everything from teaching practices, to getting started in a crafty career, to writing books to even keeping tax records. The same questions keep popping up in each class: What did you do before this? How did you start writing books? How did you get started doing what you do for a living and how can I get that job?

And I have to say, if you have to work for a living, mine is a great job to have! I can completely relate to their questions because I pondered the same burning questions at one time.

Because I've been creatively self-employed for more than fifteen years, I have a lot of information to pass on to others who may wish to take this direction. I've decided to write the book I was looking for all along—a colorful, interesting guide about living the creative life. With this book, I hope to dispel several myths about making money with your crafts. You can run a thriving craft business without involving lawyers. You can be a successful, self-employed person without being ultramotivated or a marketing genius. I want to show you what you can accomplish in a bare-bones, plain-speak, down-to-earth manner.

In these pages, you hold the collected wisdom of a group of fantastic artists who have generously agreed to share their learned expertise. You'll find their delicious words and art works scattered throughout the book. With backstories and anecdotes that are sometimes strange, often humorous but always an interesting read. You get the benefit of our missteps so your road to success will be less rocky and probably faster. To discover more about the artists, read their biographies starting on page 119.

For this venture, you need to wear several hats: designer, demonstrator, salesman, promoter of events, self horn-blower, cheerleader, writer, photographer, marketing expert, bookkeeper, psychologist, etc. The list goes on and on. You see, being an artist or craft designer isn't all there is to making money with your crafts.

There are a lot of details to be covered, and it's good to know them all. But, must you read a different book on every single one of these subjects before you even get started? No! Here's a fast, fun and easy-to-read manual with a little bit about a lot to get you started making money with your crafts.

My story

One of my earliest memories is of a brick announcement wall. Almost daily, Mom and I would walk down to the town center to study the lively collage. I was a toddler but still old enough to be fascinated by the highly textured surface made from snippets of all different sizes and colors of paper. From that moment, I saw the world as a rich, colorful and interesting place. I wanted to add to the color and to draw things as I imagined them. I also wanted to make my world more beautiful. So I put pencil to paper and attempted to create the wonder of my dreams. Many hours of my youth were spent drawing my phantom palaces I'd someday live in, my beautiful clothes I'd wear and every aspect of my anticipated life as an adult.

My art experience continued when I was homeschooled for a couple of years (while we waited for the local school to be built). Mom taught us in a very visual manner, which spurred my artful journey. We drew our own flashcards for spelling and math. It wasn't only a creative experience but also helped to permanently fix images into our memories. When we were confused

Odyssey
by Sandra McCall
PHOTO BY SANDRA McCALL

about spelling, Mom would make up a song. To this day, I can't spell *bicycle* without a rhythmical delivery.

One of my favorite classes was music appreciation. Mom would ask us to describe the pictures that the sounds of classical music generated in our heads. We'd then draw our stories with as much detail as our young minds could imagine.

Arts and crafts cornered all of my attention until young adulthood hit and I was faced with the task of paying monthly bills. Office stall, here I come. Oh boy. I dutifully held on to my jobs, spending every spare moment designing, once even maintaining a stall in a craft mall. It soon became evident that I couldn't create fast enough to stock the booth while keeping a forty-hour-a-week accounting job. But, it was also too scary to dump my day job in hopes of making a living at this already floundering craft mall. What to do—what to do…

I continued office work, until I stumbled onto the The Original Rubber Stamp Convention. This convention was all about rubber stamps, paper, inks, embossing powders and the art made with these and many more products. There I realized that there's a huge subculture of rubber stampers, and people actually make money designing images for the stamps and teaching rubber-stamp classes.

My husband and I excitedly put our pencils to paper and started our rubber-stamp company called Gains & McCall for both of our names. We drew a ton of images, designed a catalog and mailed it out. We even rented booths at a few conventions and had a small success with our line. About the same time, I started teaching at the conventions where we vended and at rubber-stamp stores. That's when I had to pick a path. I couldn't do it all; there just wasn't enough time in a day. So, I chose the path that made me the happiest. Now I teach, design stamp images and related product, write project articles and books, make DVDs and appear on television craft shows.

Before you go any further

I wrote *The Savvy Crafter's Guide to Success* assuming you want to be the sole owner of your business or with a partner. There are pros and cons to both sides of that issue, which I discuss in chapter two, "Define Your Direction." There may come a time when you'll want to form a corporation. Then you'll want to contact an attorney to explain the benefits and drawbacks of incorporating your business. There may be other reasons you want to seek an attorney as well, such as copyright issues, patents and help with contracts. In the resource section of the book on page 124, you'll find a Web site for volunteer attorneys who specialize in art and craft matters.

As you read and make plans, I want you to think about developing a legitimate business and being self-employed, even if part time. This may seem like an overwhelming thought at first, but if you make any extra cash, it must be reported as earned income at tax time. Your state's government may also want a part of your earnings, and it most certainly wants the taxes you collect from your sales. By earning money with your crafts, the government says you're in business. Whether you think it's a craft business or a hobby, it's all the same to the government.

So, think of and treat your venture as a small business from the start. It helps you keep records, track your progress, know where you need to change and stay on top of your game. Moreover, you can take several business deductions on your taxes if you call it a "business" and not a "hobby." I've always called my art career a business. Through teaching, I've traveled all over the United States and even taught at a convention in Australia! It's been a wonderful, eventful trek, but I'm not the only lucky one making money with my art. Thousands upon thousands are doing the same in one way or another and so can you.

Miss Valentine
by Sandra McCall
PHOTO BY SANDRA MCCALL

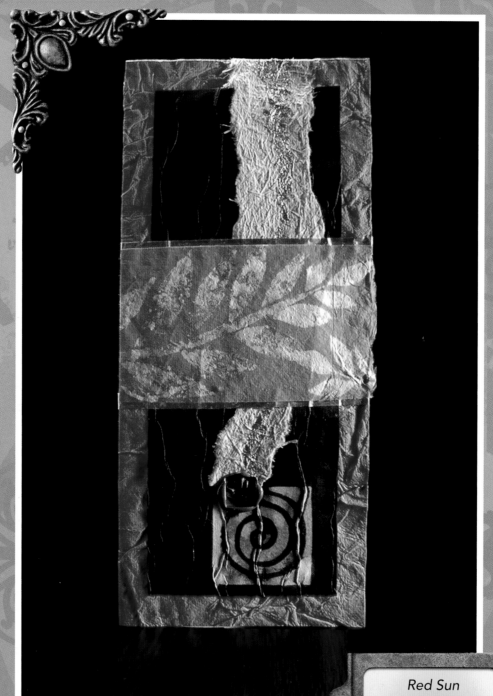

Red Sun
by Gloria Page
PHOTO BY LES GAINS

CHAPTER 1
Get Started

Taking the first step

By Gloria Page, mixed-media stamp artist

"A journey of a thousand miles begins with one step."—Lao Tzu

Taking a single small step is the key to getting to a new place. One step. Not some painful scary leap over an abyss, not something in the far distance or in the vast unforeseen future whenever you're finally ready. You take the step...now.

But "I need a better computer first."

"I can't start anything new without more supplies and I ran out of money."

"If only I had a studio, I know I could begin..."

This list is potentially endless, and it leads you down a dead-end road.

I'm going to say this as simply as I can, as simply as I try to live it: The step can be forward, yes. It can be to the side to get a different viewpoint. And guess what? Even a step back takes you to a new place because it's a perspective change. The ethereal steps are in our thinking; the next step is talking out loud, and the real steps are in our actions. I can think about writing a book forever, and I can talk about it for years. But until I sit down to write the first word and commit myself to the process, it's not going to materialize on its own. What's the art of the start? Do it.

The length of our journey in life is unknown. The more steps we take, the more we find out who we truly are and what we have that we can give to others.

"If there is no wind—row."—Latin Proverb

Some people wait for signs that the time is right. That's fine. My style is to be more proactive: I'm sitting in my own canoe, and I pick up and use the oar. Here we go.

Once you get started with your art-life, in whatever form you decide to shape it, then an amazing thing kicks into place: you have dipped your oar in the water and there are ripple effects. You can and will control certain things, and others will completely surprise you. Stay open, and the ride will take you to interesting places.

Will you always be on fire with passion and drive, able to solve any problem as soon as it presents itself? Maybe, but I doubt it. Will you face doubts and insecurities, boredom, fear and even burnout sometimes? Heaven forbid; but, yes, most likely. Do these signal the end of a dream? No. Is it time to regroup? Yes.

If someone could have predicted the future when I started my art business, I never would've believed my own story that was unfolding then and there. The experiences over the years, the connections with people, how one thing leads to another and the twists and turns that are unpredictable, the learning along the way, mistakes and victories, all of the ripple effects from staying the course and being open to how it changes over time—it's very exciting and I look forward to what is coming next.

Are you ready?

You're passionate about crafts. You want to spend every day creating. You've already given crafty gifts to your entire family, and there aren't enough birthdays, holidays or reasons left to give one more piece of your work. Your house is bursting at the seams with art you've already created, and your mind is bursting with art you'll someday create. You need a larger outlet for your creations. Surely, you can start generating some income with your arts and crafts.

Guess what, fellow crafting creature? You're born to create. Your entire body, mind and soul strive to create every single day. People ask you, "How do you get so many creative ideas? How can you come up with so many different projects?" You wonder how they *don't* have a bazillion creative ideas every single day. You know the reason you function as you do is because you *are* different. You have a precious gift. You see the world in a different way. Your mind never stops percolating creative possibilities.

Yep, you're different. Not for you is the secure nine-to-five job. You secretly resist taking orders from someone else. You hope you're not being a pest when you ask to be in charge of designing the next company catalog or sales flyer. You scan the office walls and think to yourself, *I wonder if the boss will pay me to paint a mural in the reception area. Gee, the holidays are coming up. Maybe I can make some extra money if I can get an office craft bazaar going.* You dream and you dream. But you shrug your shoulders, sigh and know you're afraid or unprepared to quit your day job.

Sure, a regular job has its perks: The paycheck, ideally, is steady. You may get health benefits. After you've gone through a certain amount of training, you don't have to think too hard about too much. You know your job. You just have to figure out how to get to work on time day after monotonous day. You also need a creative path so you don't become so bored that all your hair falls out. How can you continue to be polite and smile at your co-workers when you'd like to put a pencil through your ear the next time you have to add up another column of figures?

But, just how secure is a job working for someone else? Anything could, and often does, change in a split second. At a moment's notice and without warning, you could be out searching for a new job and starting over again. So, why not do it right this time? Why not make the choice to start earning money with your talent? You're creative! Put it to work for you!

If you could successfully earn a living with your crafts or at least supplement your wages, would you really want to?

Do you spend a lot of time daydreaming about creative freedom but worry that there are too many obstacles down that road? Do you imagine you'd love to be self-employed but think it's too scary to leave the secu-

rity of a steady paycheck? Well, making money with your crafts isn't as scary or as hard as you may have been led to believe. Just start by putting one foot in front of the other.

You've probably studied the craft scene in minute detail and spent many hours dreaming of what can be. You've gone to the shows and read countless books and magazines. Now you've brainstormed a few excellent concepts for unique gift items the buying public will gobble up. Good for you, but *thinking* and *dreaming* aren't the same as *doing*. You're going to have to develop a plan and then put that plan into motion.

J.M. Power said, "If you want to make your dreams come true, the first thing you have to do is wake up." This especially applies to anyone with dreams of turning her crafts into profits. Read this quote and make it one of the most important things you remember every single day. The truth is that great ideas are a dime a dozen. Any dreamer can come up with ideas, but dreams and ideas don't come to exist by themselves. You have to actually do the work. Picking a direction and then taking the first step is the hardest part of any adventure. Continuing the journey day by day is the second hardest task.

Being successful in the craft arena requires hours upon hours of good old-fashioned work. Many of those hours are made up of long and tedious work and "taking care of business" office work. Putting one foot in front of the other and staying mobilized make the dream a reality. It's facing your fears, your nagging doubts, your inner critic and your outer critics.

But, buck up, friend. I'm no superhero and I manage to do just that. In this book, a slew of other artists explain how they not only survive but flourish in their chosen careers. It's a lot of work. Be prepared. But the payoff for all this work is you get to do what you love. That's what makes the headache from, say, filing taxes with the extra self-employment forms well worth it. If you love what you do, then, in spite of the critics or the extra office work, you'll find a way to keep doing it.

Before you dive in headfirst, there are a few questions you need to honestly answer. This isn't just your business, but also your life. Be prepared.

Is it "art" or "craft"?

Here's how you can, and should, call yourself an artist when others may call you "just a crafter." You can already see that I use "art" and "craft" interchangeably. At some point, you'll probably feel that you get no respect for being a crafter. You might wonder if you're right to think of yourself as an artist. Why is art better or more important than craft? Is that word reserved for someone else? Maybe you already feel like this. Occasionally, you'll even have doubts about the importance of your creative contribution to the world if it's "just crafts." I know you may be afraid to call yourself an artist—to believe what you're creating is art. Well, I say, what you do is both art

One artist's journey

By Les Gains, photographer, collagraphist and sculptor

Angels Dare
by Les Gains
PHOTO BY LES GAINS

My grandfather was a musician and artist. I remember walking into my grandparents' small house. Here the warm smell of linseed oil and turpentine filled me with warmth, and I knew I'd soon see my grandfather's new painting. As I entered high school, I started playing guitar and found friends in the art department. This small circle of artists would help me realize the joy of drawing and painting.

My room was a converted garage at my parents' house. My parents allowed my friends and I to cartoon and draw at will on these walls. Ah, if only I could have saved those walls from a fresh coat of paint after I left, what a fantastic collaborative work of art it was.

After high school I found myself working for a company that made wire-bound notebooks and vinyl ring binders. This was a great learning experience. I learned about paper and its dynamic characteristics, and this is where I had my first hands-on experience in the silk-screen process. I learned how to make screens, burn images and, of course, print. This was to play a larger role in my life later.

I then started focusing more and more on playing the guitar and song creation for my various bands. My bands played the usual places, such as the Whiskey/Roxy circuit, and had our followings but never could turn the corner on the big time. I still needed cash and had a friend who was breaking into the photo business. He was working at a studio that needed help carrying lights, stands and equipment and asked if I was interested. I accepted. And from then, I was in the photo business. As time went on, I absorbed the photo world and worked as a lighting and stylist freelancer for the next six years. This was a grand time of travel, good food, creative times and good-looking people.

During this time, I fell for a young girl named Sandra McCall and we were soon a couple. This would be the beginning of a new journey in my life. We soon discovered we both enjoyed the arts. We had our dueling art tables in our once small studio and owned our first computer—a 4 megahertz 8088. On this modern miracle, we started publishing ads and equipment manuals. That was the beginning of Gains & McCall. Around this time I needed a full-time job so I found one as a screen printer and continued to be a printer for more years than I like to remember.

One of the turning points for Gains & McCall happened when we wanted to create a rubber stamp...just one. We had no idea what was out there in the world of rubber stamping. I thought it would be neat to draw something and be able to reproduce it over and over. We went to a local rubber-stamp store and asked if they could do this. From that point, we decided to start making some of our images into rubber stamps. Then it snowballed into our own line of rubber stamps. We then started working at rubber-stamp conventions selling our stamps and some of our art. Here we found a new home—one of good times, some traveling and, yes, lots of great, creative people.

Now we live in Arizona where we have a bigger studio, and I continue to work. Our house is set on a rocky hill overlooking a multihued valley holding mountains and plateaus. It's full of happy art making, hence, our new company name Arthouse525. (The "525" is for our house number.) Our new endeavors include holding our own art retreats in the old ghost town of Jerome, Arizona.

I work on things in a spontaneous manner—I don't sit down and say I will do this or that. We have a studio with plenty of supplies and I usually gravitate to sculpting, creating 3-D figures, print making, collagraphy, working with polymer plates (solar plates), soft block carving, and I still do plenty of screen printing, photography and computer art.

13

and craft. Some people have a haughty disdain for this attitude because many critics have taught us that "craft" isn't "art." All I have to say is, "Excuse me?"

True, the totally cool, never-before-seen, toilet paper cover may not be classified as "fine art." That doesn't mean it's not art, or that the person who made this "it's so simple and perfect I wish I'd thought of that" piece of work isn't an artist. In order to be an excellent artist, you have to be an excellent craftsperson. It takes time and practice to hone your skills. Likewise, in order to be an outstanding crafter, you have to have the heart and soul of an artist. You can't have one without the other. Now, you may not feel self-assured enough to say that, but without a doubt, you're an artist. If you're working every day, learning new techniques, practicing and developing your skills and you've become really good and innovative, then you can, and should, call yourself an artist. I repeat one simple phrase over and over to my students: Sign and date your work! Have pride in what you're doing. If you don't respect your work, no one will.

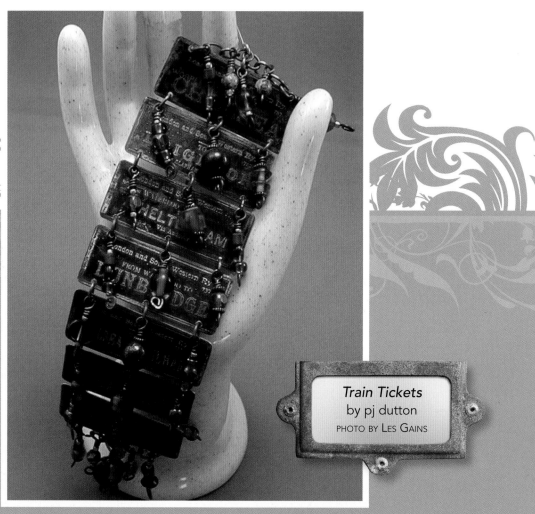

Train Tickets
by pj dutton
PHOTO BY LES GAINS

> *I know I'm an artist. I didn't have the courage to say that ten years ago. I make art...I am an artist.*
>
> **– pj dutton,** *mixed-media artist and author*

What are you afraid of?

Is your work any good, or are people saying that it's good to your face and the opposite behind your back? Will people laugh at your ideas? Are you a little too ahead of your time? Does what you're doing look great to you only? We all deal with insecurities. Doubts aren't unusual, and they aren't insurmountable. But, doubts can be paralyzing if you let them be. Without fear, there can be no daring, bravery or courage. It's true, isn't it? When you think of it that way, fear isn't such a bad thing after all.

My fear buster is to take a deep breath, close my eyes and jump in. That doesn't mean that I jump in without first being prepared. Preparation is probably the best defense against fear.

Are you thick-skinned?

Believe it or not, a common insecurity among artists who want to sell their work is fear of rejection. You might think you're the only artist who feels this way. Judging from what I've experienced, heard and read, fear of rejection is the number one reason for not starting at all, even more so than money. Does it make sense to let a fear of rejection hold you back? Everyone fears rejection. Trust me, for each time your work is rejected, you'll receive many more glowing responses.

That's not to say that rejection isn't a valid fear or that the time will come when rejection ceases to bum you out. Unless you're inhumanly insightful or extremely lucky at having the right product at the right place at the right time, rejection is a certainty. There are just too many personalities and tastes involved to have it any other way.

Rejection feels particularly personal when it's your artwork that's rejected. People tell you, "Don't take it personally." You think, *But it is personal!* For weeks, maybe months or years, you've poured all your efforts into your designs. You've finally come up with something you think is beautiful, pretty darn clever or a cool new twist on a subject, but the consumer/judge/shop owner just thinks you're off the mark. It's always difficult when others don't see things as you do, but it happens all the time.

The best defense against rejection is to prepare for it. I'm not saying you should stack on thick, titanium armor, build a big wall or walk around with a chip on your shoulder. Instead, try to view rejection as an important learning opportunity. You want to know what sells, and these people can help you. Have your questions ready so you can take this marketing opportunity and run with it. Ask why your product is off-putting. You want to know what people are looking for so you have a better chance of providing it and making great sales.

Are you prepared to live without the comfort of a steady paycheck?

This is one huge question that you must ask yourself. Understand, money will be scarce, and it will almost certainly be erratic. I believe the phrase *feast or famine* applies to being a self-employed artist more than to any other occupation.

Are you willing to be so frugal that you'll stoop to pick up just one shiny dime on the sidewalk? Believe me, that's what it often takes! What will you do if you're stiffed a payment or the check bounces? Money does roll in, but often you'll wonder when. Has everyone forgotten you? You call and call, but does it do any good? *The check is in the mail* now pertains to you and not some big utility company. You can no longer depend on a large corporation to cut you a weekly paycheck. Can you handle that?

Living the dream often means facing the hair-raising reality of not being able to pay your mortgage on time. Do you have money saved to pay your bills? To cover the bills that you've already paid? Can you manage your finances so you have funds to see you through the lean times?

Now that I've reinforced your worst fears, I'll let you in on a little secret. Most of my answers to the previous questions are no, nope and not at all. But, I have to create, so in spite of all the money worries, this is the job for me. I'm still working on managing my finances.

Are you self-motivated?

It's unlikely that you'll be able to honestly answer this question until you're tested. You may profess and profess, but you don't truly know what you'll do until you're in a certain situation. Whether you're crafting part-time or you're self-employed full-time, you're the boss in this part of your life. You can goof off if you want or you can work if you want. It's all up to you. Both the rewards and the consequences are yours to accept and embrace. How hard and how smart you work determines the outcome of your business. It's that simple.

Do you currently work a forty-hour week? Do you get up to go to work every day? On time? Then you're self-motivated as far as I'm concerned. That's more motivated than I could ever manage to be before I started this career. I always tried to be the best at whatever I did, but I must confess to calling in sick way too often. It was that getting up at the same time to go to the same place to meet up with the same people day after day that did me in. Now I make my own hours, more or less. I choose when and where I want to work and, even more importantly, with whom I want to work.

It boils down to this: If you have the minimum amount of motivation, don't worry. Trust in your art and yourself to gather all the motivation that you require to make money with your crafts. You're much more motivated when you're doing something you love.

Are you able to juggle time, deadlines and multiple projects?

"The date on the calendar is closer than it appears." I read that in a cartoon a long time ago but never found who first coined that phrase. It's so true. Proper time management can't be stressed enough. Without it, you're sunk.

When you're at an office supply store, you may wish to pick up a desk calendar or one of those dry erase

Alter Ego
by Sylvia Luna
PHOTO BY LES GAINS

I set small baby steps when it came to my art. First, I swapped art with people I admired. Next, I submitted my work to all types of zines—both print and Web, no matter how small or large. Once I conquered the black-and-white text, I began to disperse myself into the world of color magazines. During that phase, I also challenged myself to sell at a national convention. With that done, I moved on to teaching. Now my personal growth as an artist involves gathering artists in collaborative art efforts to expand their own artistic alliances. My new goal is to exhibit my work in an art gallery or exhibition.

— Sylvia Luna,
collage and altered-book artist

boards for your wall. Even though you have a day planner in your purse or a computer program to take care of dates, it helps to have something large that stares you in the face every day. That way, you're sure not to miss important dates and deadlines.

You can't afford to procrastinate when you wish to make money with handmade crafts. There just isn't enough time to do so. If you're a procrastinator, change your ways now! Make it a habit to check off jobs as you finish them. This gives you a feeling of accomplishment. When you start mismanaging time, you lose work. If you start dropping engagements or responsibilities, you lose credibility. One last bit of advice about time management: If you think something takes you two hours to complete, triple that time to look at your day more realistically.

Time management is one of my trip-ups, and it's the same with every other artist I know. We tend to think about the small things. *Oh, it only takes me twenty minutes to make a card. Why, then, does it take me so long to make my samples and mail them?* We have to look past the small stuff and add it all up. In my case, I need to make new sample boards for twelve different stores every quarter. Each store gets an average of five boards for five different classes to be presented on the new class schedule. Each board has four new cards on it and has to be assembled with the header printed and attached to it. So, four cards at twenty minutes each plus the actual board assembly time of an additional twenty minutes comes to one hundred minutes per sample board. I need to make sixty boards at one hundred minutes each. That's roughly six thousand minutes or one hundred hours of work per quarter. That's two solid weeks of doing nothing but making sample boards. Of course, no day can be filled with only one thing. There's the design time and all the daily interruptions, such as phone calls and visitors. There are the two to three hours each day answering e-mails, making contacts and scheduling the next quarter's classes and sales booths with stores and show promoters. There's the paperwork that needs to be done ideally every day, but more realistically, once a week. There's also the housework and, of course, the people who think I do nothing all day long, so why can't I just take a break and spend the day with them? All this has to be done while I'm traveling and working the current quarter's classes and artist's booths at conventions.

To top it all off, I try to work a year ahead of time to make sure I'll be able get a spot on the teaching schedules. You can see how sample boards are a lot more time consuming than just a few twenty-minute cards.

You have your own situations, and your days are filled with as many responsibilities as mine are. Maybe even more because I don't have children to feed, wash, get off to school and to spend quality time with. Your life is busy. Figure out a good time-management program and stick with it. You can't juggle it all if you don't.

As you start to get noticed, it's tempting to say "yes" to every opportunity that presents itself. That's a poor strategy. Actually, it's a lack of strategy! Artists create many extraordinary things, but no one can create time. If you've already promised all of your time to one project, you don't yet have room on your plate for another. Instead of jumping to "yes" (and later being in a position where you need to pull a rabbit out of your hat), be honest. Tell people you're busy now but will have time next week/next month/next quarter to take on new projects. Tell them you'd love to work together. That way, instead of ripping your hair out because you have over promised yourself, you appear to be confident and successful. That only makes you more attractive and probably worth the wait!

– Suzanne Lamar, *founder of craft and hobby DVD production company PageSage*

Are you prepared to travel?

You have to travel for almost every aspect of a craft business. You make a lot more money when you make yourself scarce in your hometown and travel for business. It makes sense—the people in your town may think they can take your classes anytime, so it's no big deal to wait until next time. When you're traveling, people get excited and run to your classes in case you're not in their area again.

There's more work involved if your destination is much farther than the city you live in. You have to pare down, and you have to plan. You have to decide whether to ship your class supplies and merchandise or to lug it with you.

Even though shipping is expensive, I used to ship everything ahead of time because I was afraid the airlines would lose my luggage. Then I had several bad experiences with shipping companies, and even a hotel, losing my packages. After you invest so much money in getting to your destination, it's critical that your goods and supplies arrive on time and in good condition. In all instances, I was reimbursed for the shipping and the cost of the goods, but it took six months for the shipping companies to come through. While waiting for the reimbursements, I had to buy all my supplies and materials again so I could continue teaching.

If you choose to pack goods in your luggage, thefts and confiscation at the airport are a reality even in checked baggage. (It's happened to me.) The weight restrictions are so low now that you can fit hardly anything into the cases.

I'm thoroughly familiar with every major airport in this 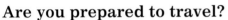 country, and that's not just a boast. At first, it's exciting to travel, but there are downsides to it as well. Flights are often canceled or rescheduled. I've spent the night in airports on several occasions. (I learned to pack an extra jacket and socks because the blankets—if you're lucky enough to get one—that airlines pass out aren't warm, and the airports are freezing overnight.) Then, I ran to my event and acted as if it was a fun and cool party, even though exhaustion was at the forefront of my brain.

Further, traveling is expensive no matter how you get there. Eating while on the road is expensive. Generally, you get paid after the fact, so you need to maintain a travel fund and pay the expenses as soon as your checks clear when you get home. Otherwise, you end up in credit card hell.

Get a passport as soon as you decide to enter this life as an artist. Exciting possibilities are ahead, and you never know where this adventure will take you. It took four months for my passport to get into my hands. Twelve to sixteen weeks is common for processing passports, and because you now need a passport even if you're flying to Canada or Mexico, it takes even longer.

Also, make sure any immunizations you need for travel are current. You may not need this to leave the country, but the United States might not let you back in if you didn't get shots ahead of time. There's a different incubation period with each shot so, do this well in advance of possible trips abroad. I didn't realize these things at first, so I missed opportunities to teach in India and South Africa.

Of course, don't forget about the home front while you're globe-trotting. You're away from home often, how will this affect your home life? Do you have an understanding someone, a neighbor or hired help who can take care of the plants, pets and kids while you're on the road?

One Man's Family
by Lynne Perrella
PHOTO BY LYNNE PERRELLA

CHAPTER 2
Define Your Direction

Finding inspiration
By Lynne Perrella, mixed-media artist, author, designer and workshop instructor

The old adage "Trust your experience" is probably one of the best creative prompts ever. Trust that the people, things and ideas that enter your realm will provide enough stimulation and subject matter for a lifetime of art making. Each fragment of an idea, conversation or image provides a nugget of information. In return, your reaction to each element sets up a "call and response" that can be used to instigate an endless flow. Art is a way of decoding information and experiences and putting them into a visual language.

Define your direction

You've got big plans and are excited about the possibilities of starting your own craft business. Before you jump right in, you need to think about the business part of this adventure. There are a number of licenses you need. What about a company name? What will you call your line? What, exactly, will you sell—a product or a craft skill? Do you need an inventory of supplies or a backlog of finished craft items? How do you get a wholesale license? Should you join forces with a friend or work alone? You might have a million questions swirling around in your head and it's easy to get confused. There are times when you may feel overwhelmed by all the minute details that go into a business.

To organize your thoughts, it helps to see them in black and white in an orderly list. Even if you think you have everything organized in your head, write it down. Forgetting is part of our human makeup, so accept it and make notes. Set up a folder on your computer or get a three-ring binder with dividers and start writing a few things down. This way, you're better prepared to put your thoughts into action. Here are a few items to take notes on as you plan for your new adventure.

Choose a solo career or a partnership

Going it alone has its rewards. You call all the shots. You're responsible for all your actions. You have total creative control over your business. The downsides are also all of the above. Another possible downside: You simply need company and don't like to work alone.

Joining up with a partner can relieve some of the stress of going solo. You have someone to man the sales booths with you. You have someone to bounce ideas off of—someone who knows your business. You can share the workload and the responsibilities while enjoying each other's company. Money can also be a motivator for having a partner.

Decide this up front, because all your decisions from here on depend on whether you need to check with your partner. For example, to start a business, you must get a license. If you have a partner, you must state your partner's name, and she also fills out part of the paperwork.

Ask other artists

Because you need to gather a lot of information about how to make money with crafts, it may benefit you to ask fellow artists about their experiences. How do they like a particular pop-up booth? Which publisher do they prefer? Have they had problems with a particular source? What do they think about a show that you are thinking about vending? Did they like working with this promoter or store owner?

Some people are ultra-secretive about absolutely everything and won't want to tell you anything. In fact, they might look at you as if they're wondering how you even dare to ask them anything at all. That's fine. Respect their position and move on. Recognize that their stance results from simple feelings of inadequacy and fear. They believe every other artist is a threat to them, so they hoard their information. And that's OK. But, don't let their closed mannerisms throw you off track.

What the fearful people don't grasp is their own actions are counterproductive to what they are trying to accomplish: making money. They haven't gotten to their position alone; they've learned a great deal from other artists. What they don't understand is we all need each other to survive and prosper. One artist, alone, isn't going to produce the rich culture of artists that prompts the world to take notice. It's the variety and abundance of art and craft that make people want to go to shows, stores and galleries and buy handcrafted items. Will the general masses spend time, effort, gas and money on a store that features only one teacher? Only if that one person is very famous. And the only way you can get very famous in your field is if there's competition. So, it doesn't make sense to worry about competition or fear it.

However, the worst thing you can do is to ask an artist to explain his techniques to you for free. Many of these artists make their living by teaching, writing articles and books, in addition to direct selling. Our talent is the only thing a lot of us have to sell. Does it seem right that you should cop techniques and designs for free—so you can go duplicate them? In this case, the raised eyebrows are fully warranted. The artists who have cool techniques have put a lot of energy into creating something unique. It is completely understandable that they don't want to share that information without payment. Your goal is to learn about making money so you may put your own style out on the market, *not* to copy what someone has already done.

I have vended several shows and not one show goes by without browsers admiring something only to put it back down and then grill me on my techniques and resources. It is annoying to say the least. You can imagine how rude that comes across, so unless you are in a classroom, technique questions are off limits. Likewise, when you go into stores or galleries featuring others' work, do not ask the store owners or clerks to explain the techniques. Do it the supportive way: Pay the store or artist for a class!

Be patient. "Interview," and I say that in a way that won't infringe on where someone else is at...it took them time, money, ingenuity and patience to achieve their goals. So, if someone else is willing to share, gobble it all up. It doesn't hurt to offer compensation in some way for their time. Read, read and read. Don't reinvent the wheel. Expect trials and mistakes and be happy to grow from them. Don't expect to be making lots of money right away. Did I say be patient?

– Stephanie Olin, *rubber-stamp and jewelry designer*

Yes, you can learn a lot about craft careers from fellow artists, but remember to reciprocate in any manner you can. Be as generous with your information as you would like others to be with you.

Pick a business name

You may use your own name for your business. That's what I do. My business is simply "Sandra McCall." Everything I do is on a name-recognition level. I teach classes, write books and sell my art at conventions. I don't feel I need a catchy name for this. You may fit into this category, too. Using your name for your business makes life easier because you don't have to file a fictitious-name statement or open a business account with your bank stating your DBA (doing business as) name.

If you want to use a fictitious name, choose a name that's unique. Avoid playing off another company's name and don't use any form of another company's catch-phrase. As clever as some of the name combinations can be, they are still derivative of another registered name, so resist that temptation. Lawsuits can and do result from name and phrase derivatives. For example, let's say Marge is in the business of sewing baby blankets using a really soft microfiber. Marge decides to combine those features and name her company Marge's Micro-soft Blankies. Even though she hyphenates Micro-soft and intends it to be a play on the characteristics of the fabric, it reads as the very recognizable "Microsoft" and that name is protected under a registered trademark. This is an extreme example, but you can see what I'm getting at here. Any litigation is usually preceded by a cease-and-desist letter. But why work so hard to make your company known to then have to start all over on your sales campaign with a new name.

According to the United States Patent and Trademark Office, "a trademark is a word, phrase, symbol or design, or a combination of words, phrases, symbols, or designs, that identifies and distinguishes the source of the goods of one party from those of others."

If you search the Internet with the keywords, "name or phrase derivative lawsuits" you'll find many examples of people who chose to use a play on recognizable names or catchphrases for their companies.

Think of a name that covers a lot of bases. For instance, Marge's Macramé can be too limiting when Marge decides to change directions in her craft. Also, think upscale. As sad as it may seem, "crafts" don't garner the same dollars as "art" does. So, instead of Susie's Crafts, try Susie's Art. Likewise, choose a name that's obvious. Frank's Fixins could be a handyman's newsletter or someone selling gourmet food items.

You may wish to register your name in your state. According to the state of Arizona's Web site, registering your business name isn't necessary, but it is a common practice. Search your state's database of operating

companies to see if your prospective business name is in use, and help prevent others from using your business name. You may also choose to register your name, labels or catchphrases with the U.S. Patent and Trademark Office (www.uspto.gov), although, it's reported to be expensive and time consuming to protect your name against infringement. However, if people search the office's files, hopefully, they'll stay away from using your labels.

If you still don't fully understand copyrights, trademarks and word or name derivatives when applied to an artist's work, visit www.medialawyer.com/lec-copy.htm#II. This site spells it out in very plain English.

Relax...then get started

Does all this business talk make you nervous? You may think that you just want to make a little extra money selling to your friends and, maybe, at a few craft shows? You want to make money with your creativity, but you don't want to run your own business? Well, once you start selling what you make, you're in business—even if you sell only once in a while. If you do this full time, then you're self-employed. Don't let this talk scare you. Running a business is the same as any other craft project—broken down into one step at a time, it can be fairly easy. As you read through this book, highlight what applies to you and make note of what you need.

One path leads to another

By Toni Curtis, doll, handmade-book and journal artist

I've always had some form of art in my life. As a child, I loved hand sewing and drawing. Although my mother had little patience for it, she taught me to sew on her sewing machine, a skill I've carried with me through my life.

In 1988, I began making cloth dolls and loved this art form. I bought books, ordered doll patterns and took classes to learn as much as possible. It wasn't long before I was hand drawing my own doll faces and painting them. Soon, I was drafting original doll patterns. I've always lived in Louisiana, so my first original doll was a Cajun Santa. Fairies and elves soon followed.

After seventeen years of making fabric art dolls, I ran into a major stumbling block: burnout. While this is usually a bad thing, in my case it was perfect timing.

Handmade books and journals had just piqued my interest. I was most fortunate to be able to attend a Bookworks weekend in Saint Francisville, Louisiana. This offered me the perfect opportunity to learn about this interesting art form. A whole new world of art opened up to me. I instantly fell in love with beautiful bookbindings and the texture of handmade papers. While chatting through e-mail, my friend invited me to participate in an altered-book round robin. I didn't have a clue what an altered book was at that time.

Soon I was running full speed down a whole new trail. I've always loved books so to be able to create my own art in them was like falling into wonderland. After amassing a collection of rubber stamps, inks, how-to books and anything else I thought I couldn't live without, fabric naturally entered the scene. I suddenly saw my fabric stash with new eyes. Painting on it, stamping on it, the options were endless. It wasn't long before my love of drawing faces and beautiful fabrics merged.

Out of a need to have a place to store drawing supplies I created my Gypsy Treasure Bag. This bag drew much attention. It was pretty but also served a purpose. I took a job at a local craft store trying to promote altered art in my area but the bag seemed to draw all the attention. Eventually, I submitted it for a class and was accepted to teach it. This was a new experience for me—it's an experience that I love.

The dolls were fun but an awful challenge to promote. While grumbling one afternoon to a friend about the dolls not selling, she responded with "This isn't how God means for you to make money." She was so right because soon after that, the wonderful world of mixed-media and alternative art entered my world.

Birdlady Art Doll
by Toni Curtis
PHOTO BY LES GAINS

My studio
PHOTO BY SANDRA MCCALL

CHAPTER 3
Organize Your Workspace

An inexpensive example from my own office

My computer office is in a small bedroom. Because my husband and I have to share office space, we emptied the room so we could start with a clean slate. We discussed how the existing furniture could be put to use. We brought our current filing cabinets, the small cabinets with drawers and the chairs into the room.

With plans, pencil and tape measure in hand, it was time to shop. Our first stop was at a thrift store where we found two long hollow doors without hardware. Then we bought an inexpensive white tabletop, four metal table legs and several large plastic bins for under our tables from Ikea. Our next stop was at a hardware store where we purchased white paint for the doors and brushed-nickel metallic spray paint for the two mismatched filing cabinets we already had.

The hollow core doors were trimmed so they were each only half the length of the wall. We attached the legs to the front of the doors—two legs per door—and attached the backs of the doors to the wall with cleats. This gave us computer workstations with legroom and storage space that spanned the entire length of one wall. The holes for the doorknobs were serendipitous as they allowed the cables from the computer setup to feed down to the electrical outlet.

Centered is another tabletop held up with two filing cabinets that come off the long workstations. The tables are arranged in a "T" shape, with the leg of the "T" extending into the room and equally dividing our work areas. Half of this long desk is mine and half of it belongs to Les.

We painted used shelves, bookcases and inexpensive storage cabinets white to make them look new again. They hold all of our materials quite nicely. With the addition of a few favorite art pieces and collectables, the room is inexpensive, clean and highly functional—exactly what we wanted.

Wasted space

As a professional craftsperson, your time is valuable. Your workspace must be organized in order for you to be efficient and time savvy. Stand back and look at the space around you. Look at every room in your house. You need an office space and a production space. Can you commandeer half of the eat-in kitchen? What about the family room or den? Do you have a spare bedroom that holds only excess belongings and a forgotten treadmill? Take a good long look at your house. Your new workspace is probably pleading with you to clear it out and make it a productive place again.

Almost everyone has wasted space—much of it eaten up by things you don't want to take the time to sell. Take stock of what you can get rid of—by selling, donating or trashing—then do it! Think of this work as a vital part of your new determination to make money with your crafts. If you have trouble letting go of useless items, think about this: What would you pay for that at a second-hand store? Be realistic. Don't think about what you actually paid. That's the past, and you want to live in the present. If you saw your item on a table at a yard sale, would you pay fifty cents? One dollar? Two dollars? Is it worth the price of the space that it's taking from your new endeavors? Will you trade this old vase for office space? Will you trade these many shoes that you haven't worn in who knows how long for office space? What about this broken chair that hasn't been fixed or used in three years? Aren't all these space eaters worth less than the money and the satisfaction you'll receive from selling your art? Let go of the past and clear some room for moving forward!

Les Gains' work table
PHOTO BY LES GAINS

I don't think organization comes easy for an artist. Organization is a habit you must develop, and it takes time. But in the long run you save time by not having to hunt for things.

– pj dutton,
mixed-media artist and author

Claudine Hellmuth's studio
PHOTO BY CLAUDINE HELLMUTH

Office space

You do need an office but it doesn't have to be expensive. An office can be highly functional as well as attractive in its simplicity. After you've cleared the space eaters and the room is empty, put a fresh coat of paint on its walls. This starts you off on the right, colorful and exciting path.

Take stock of your furniture pieces. You may have to use a mishmash of several different styles and colors. That's fine. You need to start thinking in a more frugal manner anyway. If you want to make a more pleasant workspace, it helps to unify the furniture in some way. I like to pull it all together with color. So, grab some paint and make all the mismatched pieces the same color. Choose a color that coordinates with your fresh wall color. I like white and stainless steel furniture. It looks clean and matches almost any décor. Unifying your furniture keeps the space looking tidy and, therefore, much more relaxing. And a relaxing atmosphere leads to clearer thinking, right?

Your space

Don't be afraid to reassign rooms to different purposes. It's your house—the kitchen doesn't have to be the kitchen. It can be your studio. In our previous house, the entire kitchen was our studio. The cupboards were filled with art supplies instead of dishes and food. My husband and I work, create and entertain friends and family in our small house. We took a spare bedroom for our office and the family room for our production studio. Now, the dining room serves as the family room, and the larger living room as the dining and living rooms combined.

If you want to have any type of art business, you must keep your priorities straight. I'm not saying to ditch your family. Family can come first and still live with less clutter and reassigned rooms. For instance, you don't need a formal dining room and service for twelve if only six people eat in your house. "I want to be prepared for the day," you say, "when twelve people come to dinner." That's living in the future, and you need to live in the now. Six people eat in your house now, so take six place settings and place them in storage or move them out! Look at that cake stand that takes up the room of eight dinner plates—doesn't one of the dishes do just as well for a serving piece? The bottom line is that you need space to run your business. If you set it up right from the begin-

ning, then very soon you can buy that larger house and get all twelve place settings back under the same roof.

Organized space

So you've found and cleared your workspace. Congratulations! Now you can think about organizing it. Before you can put supplies into it, you need a desk or some sort of work surface, a chair, cupboards or shelves, a filing cabinet or two and bookcases. You can make an inexpensive desk by laying a hollow core door across two filing cabinets. You can think like that for your furniture, but remember to use a unifying paint color!

Make a list of everything that you regularly use and want to keep close at hand. For your office, this includes

Sarah Fishburn's studio
PHOTO BY SARAH FISHBURN

Sherrill Kahn's
workspace
PHOTO BY SHERRILL KAHN

a computer and all the attending peripherals including a printer, monitor, fax and phone. Include paper stock and some reference books. You'll need desktop goodies like pens, pads, sticky notes, a glue stick, scissors, a metal ruler and a small cutting mat. Keep scissors, a knife, a ruler and a cutting mat on hand for trimming your newly designed-and-printed hangtags or business cards. Anything else that you need to keep in your office should go on this list.

Now that you've made a list of what you need, you're ready to run out and buy your storage containers in the right sizes. These can be as simple as shoeboxes on a shelf. Don't place often-used items in front of each other so that you have to keep moving them around to get to them. This is a huge time waster, not to mention an easy way to lose stuff. To stop temptation, buy storage containers that are large enough to fill the depth of the shelf. Repeat the same steps for your production studio and you'll be on your way to success!

Purchase office supplies wisely. It is easy to get caught up in the moment, especially when you're in the stationery store. You'll, no doubt, want all the cute little, colorfully striped paperclips, cool paper and desk accessories they stock. It's OK to buy all the office paraphernalia you feel like buying, but know this: All the little stuff adds up ridiculously fast and, all too soon, you'll wonder why you spent all that money when there is none to be seen in the months to come.

Most importantly, buy a ledger or an accounting program to record your monthly expenditures. I bought a ledger and promptly tore all the pages apart. I assign each page to one month and that page goes into an accordion file labeled from January to December to be filled as the current year unfolds. For some reason, I like the pages filled with graphite more than a computer program for keeping track of profits and losses. There isn't a thing wrong with either way except that, with a manual ledger you have to fill in the blanks on your computer when it is tax time. Incoming and outgoing monies should be entered onto an accounting program like Quicken. It ultimately saves time, since you can transfer the figures directly into your tax program without ever picking up a pencil.

For more ideas, look at other artists' Web sites. Many of them proudly put their studios on the Internet. Study their spaces; see how they organize their work areas. While you're at it, sign in and tell them how much you enjoyed their site and how you've used their cool ideas for your studio. Books and magazines are another good place to find space-saving designs that are both comfortable and functional.

The Delicate Nest
Altered Alphabet Book
by Catherine Moore
PHOTO BY CATHERINE MOORE

CHAPTER 4
Get Ready

Set yourself apart

By Catherine Moore, art-paper and rubber-stamp designer

With so many events springing up and so many classes being offered, the average person taking workshops these days is a pretty savvy consumer. They have generally taken many classes from many different instructors. With so much competition, it's important to set yourself apart from everyone else. For example, the ultimate workshop, a European retreat, would be very expensive and inaccessible to the majority. I thought it would be great to put together a workshop in which we journaled about a conceptual journey through Italy (or anywhere). One participant wrote in an online news group, "There's no one out there offering a class anything like it!"

Creating a mark that is uniquely your own is what gets you noticed. Create your own style. Submitting art and workshop proposals that were my raw, colorful unique style and not what I saw in the magazines is what got me noticed. About three years ago, a magazine editor took a workshop in Southern California. After class, she introduced herself and said she would love to feature my art in the Mélange section of Somerset Studio. Around the same time, I was accepted to be a vendor at Artfest, and that was the beginning of the whirlwind of opportunities that I have been blessed with. These opportunities opened up so many doors: I wrote my first book Collage Unleashed, *with F+W Publications; I teach at national mixed-media retreats, I write a bi-monthly column entitled "Creativity Unleashed;" my artwork has been published in various books and magazines; I've been a guest on DIY Network; I filmed my first DVD and am currently developing a product line.*

– Traci Bautista, *handmade-book and mixed-media collage artist*

Develop your image

One good way to establish yourself and get noticed in the world of art is to be published. There are books, magazines, online zines, art zines and e-zines, all waiting to hear from you. You can also team up with manufacturers by making samples for their show booths and sales information. (You'll find more information on how to submit your art and articles in chapter eight.)

There is the other obvious choice for getting noticed—advertising. All those business cards, brochures, postcards and hangtags—it's all advertising and will get you noticed. Also included in this chapter is information on two other types of advertising that may be foreign to you: the World Wide Web and television.

It just makes sense that you will be more noticeable if you have a style that is different than others. It can be your style of dress, speaking, teaching, writing and making art. Anything that you do differently will be noticeable. Developing style is part of developing your image. Style carries over to your print works as well.

Create your logo

So, how else can you develop your image? What about paper work? Every time someone looks at your business card, your hangtags or even your e-mail sign-up sheet you have a chance to make an impression. Do a little brainstorming. Make a list of every single item where you can put your contact information and logo. Part of developing your image is to make use of every single way to get your information to the masses. Here is a point list to get you started: business cards, letterheads, envelopes, postcards, thank-you notes, catalogs, flyers, mailing-list sign-up sheets, invoices, packing slips, purchase orders, labels, hangtags, stickers, information inserts (for your customers' purchases), packing material (boxes, etc.), purchase bags, display signs for above your booth, merchandise displays (think tabletops), trading cards and small giveaways, your apron or shirt and balloons for the kids. Suzanne Lamar from PageSage even puts her logo and contact information on popcorn bags filled with popcorn that she gives out at shows.

The list goes on and on.

All of this designing can be used to announce to the world your particular style and image. It's easy to design your own logos and business papers. A logo isn't necessary, of course, but it does make people remember you, especially if they start seeing it over and over again. It is easier for most people to remember visuals more than a printed line or block of text. If you don't feel up to developing your own logo or designing your business printed material, enlist the help of a friend. And, if you can, offer to pay her. We all are happy to be reimbursed for our artistic output.

When designing your printed material, keep a few things in mind: What message do you want to convey? List all pertinent contact information, including your URL, your blog and e-mail addresses, in a prominent spot. To convey your style, use a font that is in step with you. But, remember the rule of fonts—no more than three on any given piece of artwork. If you're using a crazy font, make sure that it is legible and that you use it only for the headers. You don't want to muddy the piece up and make it hard to read.

For gift enclosures and hangtags, think about putting your artistic statement on them or adding something about the item's history or interesting highlights. People love reading about their purchases and knowing special details about their context and artistry. It increases the perceived value of your artwork.

Postcards printed on high-quality, glossy photo stock may also justify increased prices. Take a few detailed and colorful images and print them onto a postcard with all your contact information. You can use these to send out in your mailings or as extra handouts for shows. Just putting them on your tabletop display can help shy people contact you.

Carry business cards with you at all times. Possibly tuck a small brochure or postcards into your purse. You never know when you'll need them. Actually, I have discovered when I'll need them the most—it's when I've run out of cards and haven't replenished the supply!

Thank-you notes are another aspect of doing business on a professional level, while adding a human touch to your image. It may make your thank- you notes more fun to send and receive if you have designed your own cards. The designs can be formal elegance, whimsical or punk art, but design them to enhance your image and your product. PageSage thank-you notes for business contacts match the rest of the PageSage marketing materials, leaving customers with even more product recognition.

Get your bio ready

It is customary for publishers and event promoters to ask for your bio. A bio is simply a condensed version of your biography, usually only two or three short paragraphs. It should include your name, your title (author, designer, artist), any education that you would like to mention and your work experience that pertains to the job that you're doing. Did a one-woman show at the corner deli last year? Write about it! Learned Web design, built your site and won all kinds of awards for it? Write it down. In other words, along with pertinent information, list your stellar accomplishments in a few, concise words. You may also include some brief contact info such as, "To find out more about McCall, visit her Web site at www.arthouse525.com."

Some people need an uber-condensed version, and they will tell you if this is the case. One magazine editor needed all her panel members to submit a bio that would be fewer than twenty-five words long. Whew! Try making yourself sound stellar in fewer than twenty-five words. Your bio is a chance for you to explain why you're qualified to do what you do. It is another chance to get noticed and to sell yourself. Make it so readers will be interested and will want to know more—so they will want to buy your art, your books or take your classes.

Writing your bio allows you to crow about yourself. This can be hard. Patting ourselves on the back does not come naturally to most of us; particularly for those who have had a lifetime's training at self-effacing behavior. It's rude to crow, right? No one likes a show off. Well, true, but sometimes, ya just gotta. If writing bios is difficult for you, try looking through the pages of just about any magazine. Most list contributor bios. Go online, check

My business logo and stationery
PHOTO BY SANDRA McCALL

My real bio

By Sarah Hodsdon, mixed-media collage, note-card and rubber-stamp designer and instructor

[When I asked Sarah Hodsdon to send her bio, she wrote a very nice official bio, but then she continued with her true feelings, and her writing was so funny that I had to share it with you. I think that many of us can relate with her on this subject.]

This is my first draft and off the cuff—I hope it will suffice and doesn't make me sound like the fruit loop I really am...wink. I always find bios pretty, well, weird. We all say stuff we know others want to hear and make us sound important and qualified; when really, in the back of our heads, we think to ourselves, Am I really qualified to do what I do? What if I just wrote, "Sarah is crazy passionate about figuring out how many different ways one person can destroy a rubber stamp and exactly what can't be altered. In the process, Sarah has learned quite a few tips and techniques she enjoys sharing with other rubber-stamping and mixed-media addicts. Her goal is to create a legion of like-minded folks to surround herself with so that (1) she can prove to her husband that there are indeed others equally neurotic and (2) she will have an endless supply of people to call when she has a 1-800-justify request (very few appreciate the fact that material only goes on sale once in a blue moon and that trinkets and trash at flea sales are now or never purchases...) Sarah's goal is to prove that you can make money doing something you're truly passionate about and is looking for other working artists who have figured out how to keep their paycheck without "reinvesting" it into other bits of trinkets and trash they don't really need but absolutely must have. As for her teaching style, if you get hit with a Nerf ball during class, it means you were slacking off and needed to refocus your attention. If your acrylic nails melted because the metal got too hot, well, that isn't Sarah's fault either. Have a piece of chocolate and add some glitter to the melted goo that once was your pricey manicure.

I took ceramics as one of my electives in my last year of high school. One day, as I was walking home from school and carrying two ceramic vases I had made, I decided to go inside a craft shop. It was a small shop that had mostly handmade items for sale. The owner saw my vases and asked if they were for sale. I was a bit surprised, but said "yes." I had no idea how much to charge so I let him make the offer. Aside from the cash he offered me, he also gave me some bottles of essential oils and told me to grab some leather scraps from a big barrel. I thanked him and continued to walk home. This was the first time I had sold something I had made, and it felt good!

– Deborah Anderson,
polymer-clay and leather artist

Pink Booties
by Deborah Anderson
PHOTO BY LIV AMES

out other artists' sites and see how they tackle this job. Check out the contributing artists' bios right here, in this book. The writing is varied, some short, some a little longer, but all interesting and pertinent.

Establish contacts

To market yourself you must establish contacts. That is how your name gets around and how you find teaching, crafting or writing jobs. Contacts can also help you out with rough spots. Sometimes you just need to vent or you need someone's advice about teaching at a particular store. You need contacts in your field to move ahead more quickly and efficiently. "Establishing contacts" just means "talking to people" and remembering their names, what they do and how you can get in touch with them. I know, I know, if you're shy, this part is kind of difficult. But, suck it up and go talk to people! You need them and they need you too.

Once you establish contacts, keep connected! When people e-mail you or send applications for you to join their conventions as a teacher or vendor, reply to them! In the beginning, I used to think that all these compa-

nies sent out mass mailings to anyone. I did not realize that these were sent to me by choice. Call it lack of self-esteem, but I really did not think they were asking me personally to be a part of their adventure, so I rarely answered back unless I wanted to participate. Now that I'm more experienced, I understand the motivation and I'm sorry that I did not reply with a yea or nay in all cases. You may be kind of a loner. I think many of us creative types are, but value your contacts! And keep them!

Build your mailing list

Collect e-mail addresses from each of your classes. Gather business cards and keep great contact info. When I started out, I was unfortunate enough to teach at a stamp store with an owner who was very insecure about losing customers to competition. And, she did not understand that I was not competition—I was the salesperson for her store. We should have been in a partnership. Well, due to that experience, I did not collect e-mails or any contact info from any of my students. This proved to be a huge mistake. If you have an e-mail list, you can let potential students know when you will be teaching at the store or will be in the area. This includes both collected postal addresses and e-mail addresses.

Building your list from event attendees allows you to make contact with people and let them know when you will be in town, when you have updated your Web site and when you have more things that may interest them.

Make a portfolio

If the idea of a portfolio worries you, just think of it as a really cool, professional scrapbook of your art. This is your chance to show your art and your accomplishments and to tell people about yourself. A portfolio does not necessarily mean one of those huge, fancy leather cases that you find in an art supply store. Many times, you will be asked to submit a mini version of your portfolio through the mail or over the Internet. For those instances, you need to make a small portfolio that you can mail or hand out to show jurors, to galleries and to other prospective clients. Of course, you will probably need to buy a nice portfolio and assemble it in the same way as your mailing portfolio—only on a larger scale.

A professional portfolio isn't absolutely necessary unless you want to get your art into a gallery. Some juried art and craft shows require you to show your portfolio if not just slides of your work. Even if you don't go into a gallery or juried show, it is good to start a portfolio that includes all of your awards and accomplishments such as getting published, being included in a museum or being the artist in the latest one-woman art show. Keep articles about yourself that may have been printed in newspapers or magazines. Keep the results from art submissions to magazines. Include the whole magazine or a tear sheet from it. Keep a running list so that you may add them to your résumé.

To put a portfolio together, you need several layers. The first is photos. Most magazines still want clear print photos or slides of your work, although many are now accepting digital photos. Likewise, most juried shows still require slides, but many now accept print or digital photos. You also need to print photos for printed material such as catalogs that you send out of house to be printed. If you're producing your catalogs via your own desktop-publishing software, then you need to use digital photos. Of course, digital photos are required for your Web site. All three types of photos will come into play in your art life, so take photos in all three forms (print, slide and digital) at the same time. That way, you're covered in any event.

You can buy a folder in the stationery store to use as your mailing portfolio, but we are artists and we want our portfolios to look semi-artsy while still maintaining a professional look and feel. That's why I nix the store-bought folders—they look kind of "grade school" to me. To make a simple but effective portfolio, take a piece of nice, heavyweight cardstock, fold it over and cut it down to make it into a 5" × 7" (13cm × 18cm) card. Some artists make 8" × 10" (20cm × 25cm) portfolios with

8" × 10" (20cm × 25cm) photos, but I prefer the 5" × 7" (13cm × 18cm) unless a juried shows calls for a different size photo. The reason? I like the look of 5¼" × 7½" (13cm × 19cm) envelopes. Seriously! No one has ever told me that the size is an issue, so I think you can be fairly creative here. The most important aspect of anything that represents you and that you want a busy person to take time to read is that it is clear and easy to peruse. I attach my business card by making small slits on the front of the portfolio so the corners of the card fit neatly into the slots.

The next layer is your artist statement. I have seen a lot of fancy statements with the longest words ever, but those don't appeal to me. Sure, it may make you sound smart to some people, but all that jargon just sounds tiring to me. And I'm willing to bet that it is also tiring to the harried gallery owner or the juror who only has a couple of minutes to browse your portfolio. So, my advice is to keep it simple.

Consider your statement as your introduction to the person opening your portfolio. It should include your goals (as an artist), your history and your medium. It should tell the reader why you do what you do and how you hope to affect the world around you. Keep it brief, only two or three paragraphs at the most. You can be slightly poetic, but try not to be too wordy or long-winded.

Next, you need to show where you have exhibited. If you've been shown in galleries or museums, list them by name and date.

The next part is optional. You may want to declare that your work is also in private collections. A private collection is one owned by a customer who's bought at least ten of your pieces. This may make you seem more impressive to the reader since an art collector has been eager to own several of your works and has paid for them.

Lastly, list your publications by name and date. This includes any television appearances, articles you have written, books and DVDs. You can also include interviews and articles that have been written about you.

There are lots of other things that you may choose to list, but remember that space is a consideration here. It's a good idea to list awards, accomplishments and grants if they're relevant to your art. You may also want to mention your hard-earned education.

A portfolio may give you more credibility to prospective clients; so include only your best work. Put your portfolio onto your Web site as well. People want to know what you have been up to.

Claudine Hellmuth tells me that she gets a lot of work by directing people to her Web site. They can see her art and her résumé with lists of all her art accomplishments there. Her Web site is professional so it makes her clients feel more confident that she will get the job done in an equally professional manner. Put very clear and beautiful photographs of your work on your Web site.

U9
by Les Gains
PHOTO BY LES GAINS

CHAPTER 5
Photograph Your Work
by *Les Gains*

A note from the author

Digital cameras, computers and printers are a boon to crafters in all areas of the creative process. With your camera, it's quick and easy to take photos of class projects or items for sale and then print them on class handouts, kit instructions, colorful postcards and flyers. It also makes it a snap to create your own advertisements that are print-ready for magazines.

A detailed photograph is especially important in preserving the memory of what you make and then sell. You'll want a record, especially if it's a one-of-a-kind handcrafted item. I also take photos of my sample boards before I send them to stores. Do this with any items you send to galleries or that are sent on any other type of consignment.

Preserve every piece of art that you make with a photo. I'm sad to realize that, in the beginning, I sent cards and art and never took photos. Now I'd like to review what I have done in the past, even if it's only to see how far I've come in my art. It's also a good idea to keep photos of your old ideas as they can generate new ideas if you ever need a little inspiration.

I use a Nikon Coolpix 2500. It's a little point-and-shoot digital camera that I love. I bought it for the macro (close-up) possibilities. Nikon digitals deliver the best close-up shots of any camera as far as I'm concerned. You can take a photo of a dime and it will clearly show every detail of the design plus any scratches and marks on the coin. I even have close-up shots of ants that are, well, pretty scary!

When I went looking for a camera, I wanted something that would allow me to take photos of jewelry that I planned on selling over the Internet. When you go into a camera shop, tell the clerk exactly what you want to use the camera for and get her opinion. It may take a couple stops in different stores, but you look until you find someone who is knowledgeable about cameras before you buy. Don't be afraid to take notes. Of course, searching the Internet will provide a ton of information about cameras, as well. The good thing about the Net is that you can get the opinions of many, many people who are happy to write about the pros and cons of each camera.

My photographs are very straightforward. I put lots of light on the project, check the angles, check for dust and lint then shoot. If I need glamorous shots, however, I turn to my husband, Les Gains.

When he lived in the Los Angeles area, Les was a stylist and a photo assistant for several photographers. He learned how to set up a shot from some of the best people in the catalog and glamour magazine industry. Our current setup is not very fancy or expensive, but very effective! We use clamp-on lights, tripods and microphone stands. Our reflectors are just large sheets of white foamcore board—nothing special but it works for us.

I've asked Les to explain his system to you, but I have one last word of my own. If you don't take good photos or you're just not interested, then hire a talented friend or a professional. The importance of excellent photos or slides can't be stressed enough when you're trying to lure a buyer with the beauty of your work, while also instilling faith in your overall competence.

Cool cameras

You have finally finished your latest and greatest piece of art, and as you stand back to admire your newborn baby, you feel that there is still more to do. Yes, you're right. The last thing that needs to be done with your work is to document it with photographs. It's not always possible to carry the history of your work around with you to show others what you have accomplished. These great creations, this evidence of your creative life, need to be seen to be sold. So, it's necessary to create a portfolio full of photographs of your work. This way you can display and transport your art without the risk of damage to the originals.

I use a Nikon Coolpix 950. It's still my favorite digital camera, though it's a little outdated. Cameras now boast several megapixels more than my Coolpix's two. With new price tags that are easily half of what I paid for mine, a digital camera should fit into your budget.

The ease of editing and previewing your images in a digital format is one of the biggest innovations to come out of the digital era. You can take pictures until you get it just right, and the only cost to you is your time and patience.

Background prep

So, let's talk pictures. I take the pictures of others' work and my own, keeping in mind that I want to represent our art in an uncluttered, professional manner. I like to start with a clean set for the photograph. The set consists of a background and a foreground. The background is what shows behind the work. The foreground is the surface that the art is sitting on. Keep in mind that the only thing you want people to see when they are looking at your pictures is your art. So, stay away from busy designs, organic fields and hi-tech-neo-classical-quasi-retro busy backgrounds. Try to stay with a neutral-toned background or go with white or black. I prefer black because it's so dramatic, but Sandra almost always prefers gray, feeling that it highlights the work without any extra drama. Either is fine. There are no rules that say you must use a particular color—it's a personal choice. Choose the background color that is suitable to your subject.

If you have a nice, large clean sheet of paper or fabric, you could use this as your background and "cove" the paper. Coving is when you drape paper or fabric from the highest point of the background down onto the tabletop, creating a sweeping flow of material so that no horizon

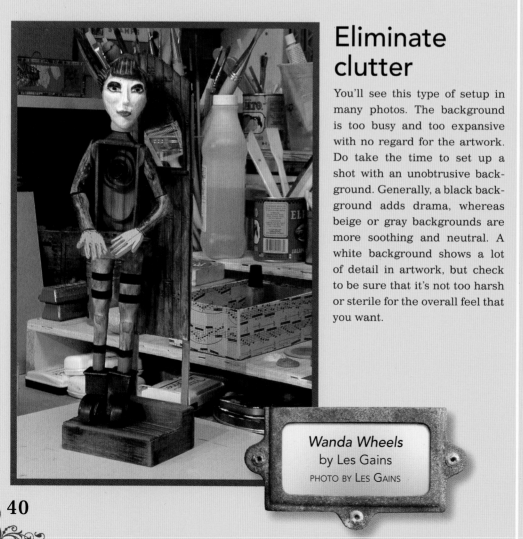

Eliminate clutter

You'll see this type of setup in many photos. The background is too busy and too expansive with no regard for the artwork. Do take the time to set up a shot with an unobtrusive background. Generally, a black background adds drama, whereas beige or gray backgrounds are more soothing and neutral. A white background shows a lot of detail in artwork, but check to be sure that it's not too harsh or sterile for the overall feel that you want.

Wanda Wheels
by Les Gains
PHOTO BY LES GAINS

Watch positioning and lighting

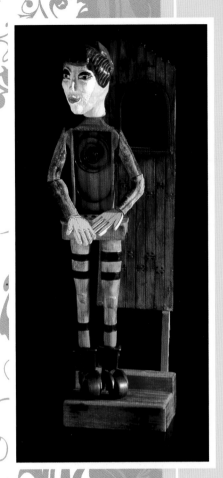

There are two problems with the shot on the left: the position of the subject and the lighting. The face is turned so it looks out of the picture, which draws the viewer's eyes out of the photo as well. Also, the doll is lit on one side with an incandescent lamp with full bulb exposure. This lighting makes the picture too yellow, too contrasted and too "hot" on the side facing the lamp. The hot side causes a glare, which detracts from the details of the piece. The lighting also causes a loss of detail on the shadowed side.

For the picture on the right, I turned the doll's head so that it faces into the picture. Another lamp was added to the opposite side of the doll to balance the light. Now you can see detail in the shadows. I placed sheer fabric panels in front of the lamps to diffuse the lights. This was to avoid the hot spots and to show more detail on the doll, especially in the white face.

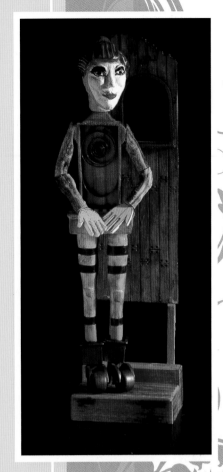

Wanda Wheels
by Les Gains
PHOTOS BY LES GAINS

line shows between the foreground and background. You can achieve some nice falloff of light that will highlight your piece even more. Falloff is when the light in the foreground of the picture fades to dark in the background. Also remember to keep the area within the picture as clean as can be. Try to be meticulous with your efforts. You don't want to see dust on the tabletop or pieces of string trailing out of your picture. Keep it tight and clean.

Art prep

You don't want to just throw art onto the table and take a photo of it; you need to "dress it." One of the biggest problems I see when looking at pictures of people's work in books and magazines is that they don't take the time to make the handcrafted item look as good as it could. If you have tags, or ribbons, or doodads that hang off your piece, make them look presentable by making sure they hang in a natural, gravity-oriented manner. Do not let your ribbons tangle around each other. The last thing you want is a picture that looks as though you just pulled this piece out of a drawer and started snapping photos.

Small items or fibers hanging from artwork may be an integral part of the piece. However, they can present a problem in arrangement. They need to hang so that the point of interest is visible to the lens. If you don't make this happen, you'll end up seeing the backsides of tags and weird shapes that are out of context with your idea. This creates a distraction and it compromises the choices that you, the artist, made when the piece was first created.

After you have arranged it, look at the item through the viewfinder. Are there weird spaces between elements of the art? Weird spaces are monopolizing spaces. They will be the first things that catch your eye when viewing a photo. Your goal is to highlight the art and not the negative spaces around it.

The same critical look must be given to leaves, flowers, papers and every part of the item to be photographed. Make sure none of the elements are crunched up or smashed unless that is your intention. If you're shooting art for someone else, make sure the work is right-side up. Sandra complains all the time about

Use fill cards

This shot has a lot of drama because only one light was placed to the side and a little to the front of the doll. To fully show the artwork, there should be more detail in the shadows. Balance the lighting by placing another lamp opposite the first as I did in the #2 shot on page 41. To keep a little more shadow and still get detail, place a "fill card" on the opposite side of the lamp, which bounces light from the lamp back onto the subject. A fill card can be as simple as a large piece of white foamboard.

Wanda Wheels
by Les Gains
PHOTO BY LES GAINS

magazines shooting her work upside-down even though she clearly marks the back of each piece. To be fair, that may be more the fault of the production department than the photographer.

Also, keep in mind that most of the time your work will look more dynamic if you show it in a three-quarter view as opposed to just straight on. You want to show that it has depth as well as height. A three-quarter view shows the front and some of the side at the same time. So if you're taking a picture of a card, you want the front to show, but try giving it a little bit of a twist to show that it's a folded piece and not just a flat piece of paper. You should try this on all of your shots, knowing that not all subject matter is suited to the same angles and that there will be times when a three-quarter view just won't work for the piece. Shoot several different angles so you have a large number of photos from which to choose the very best.

When you're shooting flat cards or flat artwork, try using "lifts." Place a piece of wood or plastic, or whatever you have available, underneath your art piece,

lifting it off of the tabletop. Then, get onto a ladder and shoot straight down onto your subject. This will add depth to your flat artwork and will pull it away from the background. You can get cool drop shadow effects this way as well.

Lighting

Very few of us have access to a professional lighting system of strobes that can be adjusted for different f-stops, softboxes, lighting stands and a degree from a prestigious photography school plus all the other toys that money can buy. But you can take pictures that look professional if you take your time with the lighting.

The first step toward good lighting is to disable the flash that is attached to your camera. The light from the camera flash generally creates what is called a flat image. This means there's very little shadow or edge detail on the art. There's probably a very harsh, dark shadow behind the art and a hot spot, an area where it's so light that you see no detail, on the front.

Even though you may not have an expensive, professional lighting system, there is an easy way to set up the lighting that will make your picture interesting, dramatic and dynamic. Start with a darker background color like black or gray. Set the art onto the display surface.

It helps to pull the drapes across the windows to eliminate unwanted light. Grab a table lamp that is not taller than the subject. Take the shade off and use that as your main source of light. I use a 75-watt tungsten light bulb. This is plenty of light for what I have been shooting. Do not use fluorescent lights because they cast a green tone. Tungsten lights, which are your everyday, household light bulbs, cast a warm orange type of light.

There are differences in household light bulbs too. Check your hardware store for a bulb that's labeled "true color" or "daylight." That is what you need to buy for your lamp. Place the lamp next to the art and then step back to take a look. Make sure your household lighting system is not casting a strange color onto your work. You may need to change the light bulb a couple of times until you find the one you like.

Most new digital cameras have the ability to adjust for the light source. This setting is your "white balance," and you may need to adjust it to get the most natural looking light you can. If the overall tone in the final photo is too yellow or too green, you can further tweak the picture in an image-editing program such as Adobe Photoshop.

3-D artwork
Place the table lamp to one side and a little in front of the object. This will create nice shadows across the front giving it depth and dimension. You must decide how dramatic you need your piece to look. It takes a little time to play with the lighting, but it's worth it.

Light from the lamp bulb can be directed by bouncing it off white cards or boards. Prop the board by taping it to a tall bottle or jar, control shadows by directing bounced light onto the subject.

Minimize the light that is falling onto your background by blocking the light coming off of the lamp. In other words, by placing a card on the back of your light source, you can prevent light from hitting the background and this will make your piece of art stand out.

Disable the flash

When taking photos of artwork, you should always disable the flash on your camera. In this photo, you see what happens when you leave the camera's flash on. The black background and dark table don't blend and show every wrinkle and speck of dust. The subject is overexposed and flat with the white face almost completely disappearing.

Wanda Wheels
by Les Gains
PHOTO BY LES GAINS

Eliminate shadows

In the photo on the left, the figure is placed against a pale yellow background and shot with a flash. Note: This method may produce dark shadows behind the art. To avoid this, disable the flash on your camera and set up proper lighting.

Another way to light a figure and add drama is to place your light source above the subject as in the photo on the right. There's no camera flash with the yellow background so you don't see harsh shadows behind the figure. The lighting is dramatic, but you still see detail in the artwork.

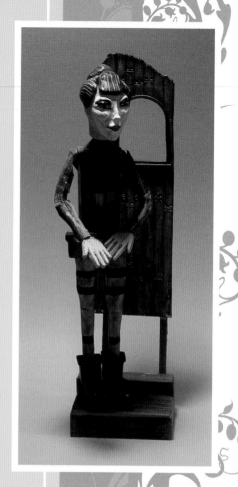

Wanda Wheels
by Les Gains
PHOTOS BY LES GAINS

Try to place your blocking card so that it doesn't create a harsh shadow line. Sometimes you have to play with this to find the correct angle. This also takes time. The more distance you place between your blocking card and your light source, the more feathered the light that does fall onto your background becomes.

Now that you have a light source only on one side of your artwork, you need to fill in light on the other side. You can do this by placing a white card or board opposite your light source. This bounces the reflected light back onto your object. Make sure the size of this "fill card" is big enough to light all of your work. You don't want the fill light to cover only the bottom part of your piece or just the top, because that might look a little odd.

The light being cast from your fill card softens the shadows created by the main light and throws more light onto what would be the darkest side of the image. This allows you to see more detail in the shadows of your piece but isn't bright enough to flatten the image. The light coming off your fill card is not as intense as the light coming from your lamp (the main source). So you can start painting with light, manipulating the highlights and shadows as you go.

If you can, suspend another lamp above and a little bit behind your subject. Light from above and behind gives your object edge lighting; it gives a little glow to the top edge, separating it further from the background. Do this by taping a clamp-on lamp to a "boom." To make a boom, position a broomstick so that is comes off a ladder and is suspended over the artwork. Use duct tape to attach the broomstick to the ladder and then add the clamp-on light.

If your light sources are too harsh or overpowering you can back them away from your subject a bit to change the strength of the light. Remember, as you move the light farther away the light is cast in a wider pattern, so watch the light on your background. Try placing a piece of tracing paper or parchment paper in front of your light to diffuse the light and give you a softer light than the bare bulb.

Flat artwork

Shooting flat artwork is less complicated although you still have to watch closely how you use your lights. For flat artwork you need a flat light source. Use two lights placed at equal distances from each other on either side of the camera and in line with the lens. Again, this is not carved in stone but is only a starting point. It seems like you always have to move stuff around. Make sure the cast light does not create hot spots on the artwork. Hot spots are where the light is so strong that it glares and shows no detail in the final photo.

Natural sunlight

Naturally, you can take your work outside or shoot close to a window where the sun is streaming in. There is nothing wrong with using sunlight as your light source. However, since the sun floods everything, everywhere, you're generally guaranteed a flat natural light, meaning that it will be harder to control the shadows and highlights on the art. If you're shooting by a window, make sure there are no weird reflections being cast on your image. But, do try some natural light photos at different times of the day. Sometimes that is exactly the light you need.

Camera supports

Supporting the camera is another important concern. You can have a million-dollar camera, but if you don't support it so that there is no movement, you end up with a million-dollar fuzzy picture. So, use a tripod. Use a tripod. *Use a tripod.* Even the least expensive tripod you can find will help you take a sharper picture. Even if you have hands of steel there is a good chance that your photo won't be as sharp as you might have hoped if you don't use a tripod.

When you mount your camera to a tripod, you can shoot the picture using a cable release, but a lot of cameras don't have this capability. The next best thing to do is use the self-timer found on your camera. This is the feature you use to get yourself into the group shots—the ones where you click the self-timer and then you run around and join in on the picture. When you trigger the camera to expose the shot, you risk wiggling the camera just enough to make a blurry picture. When you use the self-timer, the camera has time to stop shaking and settle down.

Lighting and eliminating movement are the primary objects of this game.

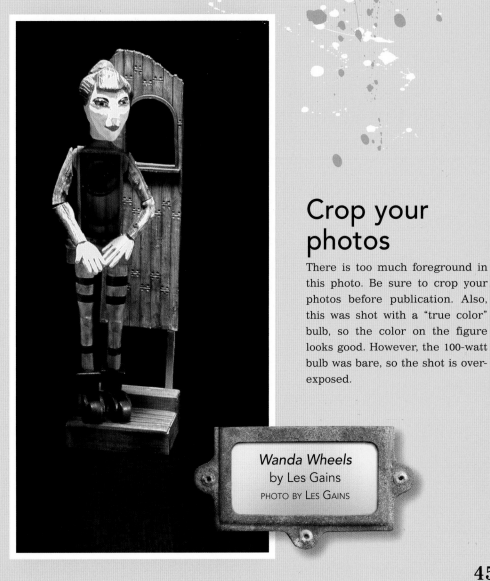

Crop your photos

There is too much foreground in this photo. Be sure to crop your photos before publication. Also, this was shot with a "true color" bulb, so the color on the figure looks good. However, the 100-watt bulb was bare, so the shot is overexposed.

Wanda Wheels
by Les Gains
PHOTO BY LES GAINS

Self-Portrait
by Sarah Fishburn
PHOTO BY SARAH FISHBURN

Try not to be shy or too self-effacing. Let the world know you're making art! Let them know you would love to provide them with the perfect piece to meet their next art need, whether that's a gift or some little something just for themselves. If you don't point yourself out, no one may ever realize you're here!

– Sarah Fishburn, *collage artist*

CHAPTER 6
Get Noticed
by Suzanne Lamar

by Suzanne Lamar

A note from the author

You need to let people know that you're here and ready to create something special for them! There are lots of ways to advertise, one of the most effective being word of mouth. Talk yourself up! Once you start, others will jump in and help you get the ball rolling.

My friend Suzanne Lamar has a better head for advertising and marketing than anyone else I know. I asked her to share her insights with you. Suzanne had so many good points that I am including all of them for your enjoyment.

Know your market

You might have the most amazing product, idea or technology on the planet. That's great news! The bad news is that if you don't spread the word, no one will blindly discover you and pay you. You need to spread the word and get noticed. Where do you begin? Who should you talk to? Who is your ideal customer? As a group, we all may want to make money for our art. Individually, however, we may have very different customers.

• Do you sell original artwork (e.g., paintings, clothing or jewelry)? The ideal customer here may be the individual who purchases art for resale.

• Do you design products? The ideal customers for designers may be art supply manufacturers.

• Do you teach classes at stores, conventions and/or retreats? Here your customers are the individuals managing these events: store owners, event planners and large art supply manufacturers.

Many artists have more than one ideal customer. Maybe you teach workshops *and* design products. That's even better! Each type of customer needs you to communicate in different ways. No problem. We already know how to do that. We tailor our communication for a variety of audiences every day. Think about a significant event that has happened in your life. Would you tell the story of an event in exactly the same way to your parents, your spouse, your children and your co-workers? I doubt it. Different audiences want to hear different sides of the same story. Communicating in business is the same thing; we need to tailor our message to the desired audience.

Aim high

As you think about your ideal customer, some key industry visionaries may come to mind. Who are the contacts you would most like to meet professionally? Your A-list should be short. These are the handful of people that have the resources to boost your business to the next level.

Carol Duvall was on my A-list the moment I entered the hobby and craft industry. *The Carol Duvall Show* was the highest-rated show on HGTV for ten years. As the host, Carol showcased the best products, artists and projects in the industry. She's introduced more people to crafting than any other individual. Clearly, she has a unique perspective and experience that would benefit any company in the hobby and craft industry. Carol may not be the best person for your personal A-list, but you get the idea. Aim high.

Develop your elevator pitch

What if you get to meet someone on your A-list? That first encounter will probably be brief. You may only have a shared elevator ride. You need to be able to make a memorable impression quickly. What would you say in those precious thirty seconds? In that moment, you may be so excited that you can't find the right words to get the ball rolling. The key is to craft your best introduction now. My current elevator pitch is: "My company produces award-winning instructional DVDs for the hobby and craft industry."

That's it. One sentence. Well, I admit that sometimes I do add a bit more: "Hello. My name is Suzanne Lamar. I'm with PageSage. We produce award-winning instructional DVDs for the hobby and craft industry."

That's the most I tend to say when I can introduce myself to someone I don't know in a business setting. If they ask me a question, I keep my answers short and focused until they ask for more. With this strategy, I'm polite and confident instead of pushy or desperate.

Practice your elevator pitch whenever you meet a new person. The goal isn't to be overly clever here. This is the wrong moment to discover that the other person has a lousy sense of humor or is easily offended.

What if the other person isn't interested in your pitch? Look him in the eye, tell him to have a good day and move on. There may be a chance later in life where you have something more compelling to tell this person. Later, if he remembers you from your initial meeting, the only memories he will have will be positive ones.

Time your introduction

When is your customer most receptive to what you want to communicate? This is basic stuff. If I asked you to dinner and you wanted to go to a specific restaurant, you should tell me that before we go to a different restaurant. Telling me after we've been seated in a different restaurant could be worse than not saying anything at all. I'm either going to wonder why you did not feel comfortable enough to tell me in advance, or I'm going to feel bad

Type of Customer	What They Need to Know
Individual consumers	Where they can buy your work Retail prices for your artwork Where they can meet you
Businesses	How they can purchase your work (e.g., buying outright vs. reselling vs. selling on consignment) Wholesales prices for your artwork Reorder process
Manufacturers	Type of business arrangement you desire (are payments computed hourly, per piece, or a royalty arrangement) If designs are exclusive to the manufacturer Do you design for any competing companies
Event-based representatives	Do you provide samples in advance to help market the event What hours will you be on site

> *I rarely send out e-mails unless I'm promoting someone else's workshop at my place. Usually people just browse my Web site to find out the latest.*
>
> **– Sylvia Luna,** *collage and altered-book artist*

Archives
by Sylvia Luna
PHOTO BY LES GAINS

that I did not pick something that pleased you. Neither of these impressions makes me feel good. People don't like to do business with people who don't make them feel good. In some instances, the best time to communicate with your customers is obvious. Trade shows are events where people are actively seeking the latest information about a particular industry. Other times you just have to pick up the phone and create good timing.

When I call someone for business, the conversation typically begins the same way:

They: Hello?

Me: Hello. This is Suzanne Lamar from PageSage. Did I reach you at a good time?

Telephones are intrusive. I rarely have someone call me the moment that I most want to talk to him or her. I answer the phone because it's ringing, not because it's the best time for me to chat.

Most people believe that if they reach you on the phone, they should never turn down the opportunity to make their pitch. That isn't true. People are even more receptive to your message if you begin with great manners. If they can't talk at the moment, ask when it would be a good time for you to call back. Thank them and tell them that you look forward to talking to them at whatever time or day they requested. When that appointment time comes, call them back. Now, just because you have an appointment does not guarantee that their day is on schedule. So, reintroduce yourself. Remind them that you called yesterday, last week or whenever. Ask them if this is a good time to chat. If not, repeat these steps until they take the time to chat with you. I've had

some people eventually make time to talk to me just because they were impressed with the patience, courtesy and diligence I demonstrated in making an appointment to chat!

Tell people what you want

Congratulations. You now have the attention of your desired audience. If you have not uttered it yet, start with your elevator pitch. If you're meeting someone for the first time who already knows something about you, you may decide to tailor your elevator pitch. The first time I ever met Carol Duvall, coincidentally, I went to The Carol Duvall Show with Sandra McCall where she was doing a guest appearance. I knew that Carol knew about PageSage. So, I tailored my introduction:

"Hello. My name is Suzanne Lamar. I'm with PageSage, the company that produced Sandra's DVD."

Now tell them what you want: "If you are ever interested in creating a DVD, I'd love to have the chance to work with you."

I did not yet have a clear concept concerning what kind of DVD I might produce with Carol Duvall. I just knew that if she was thinking about making a DVD someday, I wanted to her to know that I was available.

A lot of people fear rejection so much that they are afraid to ask for what they really want. I don't look at the word "no" the same way as these people do. If someone tells me "no," I have not lost anything. Clearly, "yes" is the best outcome when you ask for something. But "no" isn't a bad thing. In fact, I like "no" because it's a time-saver. "Maybe" means that I should keep in touch and try again to see if it could become a "yes." With "no," I can scratch that person off my list and focus on the next contact who could help me achieve my objective.

Create a consistent look

Whenever you put your message in writing, appearance is just as important as content. All of your marketing material needs to have a consistent look and feel to it. Pick a color palette, a font or two and a style. Then stick with it.

People often associate what they see with the message so much that they can't separate the two. Would you recognize a UPS driver if he didn't drive a brown truck and wear only brown clothes? People notice something that becomes familiar: the chef's coat or the color brown. That is how they recognize you. Create a consistent look for how you present yourself. If your printed pieces don't have a unified look to them, they can feel scattered and disjointed. That isn't good. Customers will think that you're scattered and disjointed as well! Consistency doesn't have to mean boring. Take a theme and tweak it a bit each time.

Build an image

PageSage developed a theme as a first-time exhibitor at CHA (Craft & Hobby Association). This is the big international wholesale show for the industry (and one of the one hundred largest trade shows in North America). PageSage produces DVDs. DVDs aren't large objects. To create a presence at this show (and to stand out from the other hundreds of exhibitors), you need to occupy some space. A 10' × 20' (3m × 6.1m) booth felt like the right size. But the entire PageSage library at the time could fit in the palm of your hand. If PageSage merely filled the booth with DVDs, it would be cluttered instead of inviting. Naturally, we wanted to play the DVDs in the booth. To do that, we could have used a few folding chairs and a TV screen with a DVD player. From a functional standpoint, that would have been both cost-effective and utilitarian.

But that wasn't the image we wanted to create. Instead, we created a movie theater. We found some wonderful vintage theater seats on eBay. We bought some inexpensive film reel tins and asked each of our artists to decorate one. (They, in turn, created some real masterpieces!) Now that we had a theme, it became simple to determine what did or did not fit the theme we created. Everything in the booth reinforced the theme. We rented a popcorn machine and gave popcorn away to everyone who walked by. Popcorn worked for us because it supplemented our theme. Plus, it has a distinctive sound and aroma that made attendees come and look for us.

If something is blank, print on it. We had the popcorn bags custom printed. That way, when people walked away from the booth munching on a snack, everyone else could see where they got it. We included the company name, our marketing tag line and the booth number along with a graphic of a movie theater.

We designed a uniform for everyone working in the booth. For our theme, we wanted to look like movie ushers with black slacks and custom white shirts. Uniforms make it easy for customers to know whom to talk to for more information. Your group looks and feels like a team. PageSage shirts share the same graphic found on the popcorn bags. It's all part of the same whole.

The movie theme is further reinforced on the PageSage Web site as well. Head silhouettes against a filmstrip are the main navigational design element at the top of each page. The blue filmstrip background used here is also the background used on the cover of the current PageSage catalog. Tie it all together and you make it easier for your customers to notice you.

Design the product's look

If you're designing a line of products, then you also need to create a consistent look for your packaging. As customers become familiar with your product (and, ideally, totally fall in love with the product and want to purchase other items from you), you want your products to be instantly recognized as part of the same company. PageSage DVD covers were designed with these principles in mind. PageSage covers share some common design elements:

• The company name (both as part of "PageSage presents" and www.pagesage.com) appears in the same location on all covers. The same font is used for this text on all covers.

• Each cover has a strong vertical semi-transparent strip along the left edge that wraps around as the spine background color. There are also two horizontal bars in the same color that always appear in the same position.

• An art supply list appears in the foreground in the lower left corner. This is typically a tool or product used by the artist on the DVD.

• Text on the spine is always in the same font and position. The PageSage logo appears in the same position on each spine.

• The inside of each DVD lists all of the products used, by project, throughout the DVD.

• The inside of each DVD includes a photograph of artwork from each technique and/or project shown on the DVD.

Stand out

Newspapers, magazines and television news all have one thing in common. They need new information to package and distribute to their customers (i.e., readers, viewers or audiences). So, if you have a compelling message they may help you spread the word. Other people and companies are competing for their attention as well, so you need to figure out how to get noticed.

At the CHA Winter show in 2007, one hundred forty-six companies provided press kits for the press room. That is a lot of information for the press to sort through. (All in all, CHA estimates that they received 18,000-19,000 total press kits.) PageSage had a big product

announcement to make and this was the best place to do it. We had to get noticed!

Six months earlier Sarah Hodsdon and I walked part of the CHA Summer show together. (I'm sure you have seen her artwork gracing the pages and covers of various craft magazines. You can also see her work throughout this book.) We discovered that CHA presents an award for the best press kit at each show. So, when it came time to craft our press kit, I asked Sarah if she would work with us to design an award-winner.

We talked a lot about ways we could take our theme and translate it into a compelling press kit. Sarah amazed us with her creativity and ingenuity. She photographed a beautiful old theater. With a bit of Photoshop wizardry, we customized the theater name and marquee. We also removed some people who were loitering in front of the theater when the picture was taken. Sarah found a clever way to use both the look of PageSage printed pieces and the feel of the PageSage booth and to communicate that visually on the cover of the press kit. It was a home run. PageSage was awarded the Golden Press Kit award as the best press kit of the show.

Build a community

The press kit story leads to another important point. No one is an island. We all have a team of people behind us as the wind beneath our wings. When you first start a business, those cheerleaders are likely your family and friends. To grow a business, though, you need to build a community of other people who work in the same industry and share your vision. Networking with other people is key. In the press kit story, PageSage won because by winning the award, there was a buzz at the show about our press kit. People sought out the PageSage booth to learn more about us. This was also a win for Sarah Hodsdon. In that moment, Sarah became an award-winning designer. Other companies that would like Sarah to design their press kits for next year have already approached her!

Listen

People enjoy talking about themselves and will tell you all kinds of interesting stories. Listen. Don't just listen for the pauses where you can jump in and say something. Listen to the stories and the details. Pay attention to what people don't do as well as what they do.

I wanted to produce a DVD with Carol Duvall. Our paths crossed a few times every year at different industry events. She liked PageSage DVDs. She always rec-

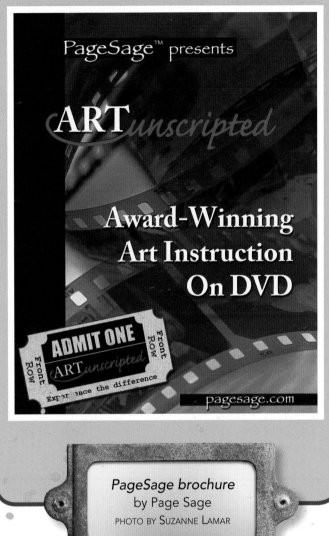

PageSage brochure
by Page Sage
PHOTO BY SUZANNE LAMAR

ognized me and had something nice to say. But she never took me up on the idea of talking about doing a DVD together. How do you interpret that? Maybe she just hated the idea of doing a DVD. No. That did not make sense. She wasn't camera shy. Carol Duvall invented crafting television! When the idea hit me that she would be perfect to host an event for PageSage (that we also wanted to film and release on DVD), I had an epiphany. I had missed the point. It was not that Carol didn't want to create a DVD. The issue was fit. I finally had a full concept to share with Carol that perfectly fit her expertise. She is the ultimate craft hostess, and that is exactly what this project required. Carol was delighted to be asked and agreed to do the project.

Final word from the author

Through the years, I've discovered the importance of advertising both as my company "Sandra McCall" and my expertise as an artist. I discuss selling yourself as a teacher and writer in the following chapters. Here I start with a few ways to advertise your business.

Television

Network television ads are expensive. We've all heard about the millions of dollars paid for ads that run during the Super Bowl and just assume that we are priced out of the TV market. Believe it or not, all television advertising isn't expensive. Some local television stations have low cost advertising time slots. Often, they will have unsold time slots and they can insert your ad for relatively little money. Contact your station to see what their policies are. I know of one rubber-stamp store owner who advertises her store, in this way. It makes perfect sense because the local crowd is the primary crowd that she is trying to entice into her store so why not grab their attention when they are watching TV? Rhonda DeCandia shares her thoughts on television advertising: "Anyone can call their local TV or cable station and ask for the advertising department.

"When we first started I told my rep how much I was willing to spend, and on which channels we wanted to focus. Generally, a sales rep should have a good idea of which channels will work for your industry. For our store, we focus on showing the ad during The Carol Duvall Show or other craft shows since so many of our customers watch them.

"Advertising is so important and one of the areas stores really neglect. Our ad has been running for more than two years and we still get new customers from it, even people who have lived here all along, but

Journal
by Traci Bautista
PHOTO BY MICHAEL VINCENT

To be successful and make a living as an artist you can't forget the business of art. It's essential to have a Web site, blog, MySpace and e-mail newsletter to promote your work, events and products. Don't be afraid to let the world know what's going on with you and your artwork. I am not only an artist, but I wear multiple hats: author, TV personality, Web designer, marketing director, product designer, accountant, travel agent, event manager, business developer, publicist, writer and technical troubleshooter.

– Traci Bautista, handmade-book and mixed-media collage artist

never noticed the ad before. Also, because we run ads regularly we get a number of 'free' ads from the unsold spots. So our ads show up all over the place."

Web sites

When I look for products or services these days, I almost always go to the Web. If I want to find out about a certain artist, I go to the Web. If I need information on just about anything at all, I search the Web. I, along with many others, rarely even pick up a phone book anymore. Even when I do go to a phone book, I look to see if a Web site is listed and then I go check out the site before calling or driving to a business.

These days, having a Web site is just as important as having a business card. There are numerous options available for creating a Web site. You can select a relatively inexpensive option or invest in a robust site full of scintillating audio and video. The mechanics of how to create a Web site are better suited to a different kind of book. The point I want to make here is that you may be surprised by how many customers will initially discover you on the Internet. For those customers, if you're not on the Internet, it's as though you don't exist.

I can generally find what I need on several different sites. The people whom I choose to do business with are the ones whose sites I like the best. It may not be the wisest way of doing business, judging a company by it's Web designer, but it's my way and the way of a lot of other people, too. It really does make a point for good site design if you're trying to gain business or to get noticed as an artist. Your Web site must be attractive and easy to peruse. Most importantly, it must load fast! I read somewhere that people who are surfing will give you three seconds to see what your page is about. Three seconds! If your page does not load immediately, they are off to another site. If you're not good at or don't understand Web design, there are plenty of Web hosts that provide professional templates. You choose your colors and plug in your information and photos—it's as easy as that.

There is a learning curve to building a Web site, so it can take some time. Maintaining it is another chore and can be quite a time burner. I cannot imagine someone else in charge of my site though, so I bought Microsoft FrontPage, a couple of books and learned to write HTML code. If you don't think this is for you, hire someone to do this for you. Check out a few sites and ask around for a Web master. You can find the names of Web masters listed at the bottom of their sites. Contact them—they may be too busy to pick up another client, but at the very least you will make their day by telling them how much you admire their work.

OK, so, you've built your site, but will they come? Not if no one knows about it. No matter how fascinating your Web site is, people need to know about it and they must want to visit it. That means you should also advertise and promote your site—a lot! You can do this by putting your Web address on all of your correspondence, business cards and advertisements and on all contact information you include with magazine articles and books. Send out notices about updates and new information posted to your site. Link and be sure to ask for cross-links with other sites as well. This will drive more visitors to your site.

Blogs are another way to get more people to check you out. Choose a blogging site and hop on. They are very easy to set up and, best of all, they are free. I chose www.blogspot.com because of an article that I read online from Wired magazine.

Put your stamp on You Tube (www.youtube.com) as well. Except for your time (and I know that your wage is about three cents an hour if you're an artist) it's more almost-free advertising. Search the Web to find out more information about all of this technical stuff.

Magazines

Most magazines have a section that is all about new products. If you develop something new, send a sample with a full write up about the item. Include the item description, price and all of your contact information so that people may order it from you. Years ago, when I first started stamping, my husband and I came up with a unique rubber-stamp positioner. We sent it to several magazines, and we received orders for it! It was as simple as that. Magazines are always on the lookout for new items and are happy to hear from you.

True, magazine advertisements can be pretty expensive. A small, one-twelfth page ad will run you around $125 to $300 for a major publication. You're responsible for layout and all the information contained therein. You must also meet the publication's deadlines set forth in your agreement. All magazines have a section where they list the editor's names and all the pertinent information. You can find the advertising sales department listed in this section. If you contact them, they will mail you a folder with all their criteria spelled out. Their job is to sell advertising space so they are very nice and not scary at all to talk to.

Newspapers

Newspapers and some magazines handle news releases. If you do something interesting (if you come up with a new product or if you're doing something special in their neck of the woods), write up a news release. Include a photo of either you or your product. Be sure to include the date that you want the publication to release your news. Call or e-mail your papers to see how they would like you to submit press releases. Many of them accept e-mail notices. All of them are looking for your story so most are polite and helpful and not scary at all. Send it in! You have nothing to lose and a lot to gain.

There are people who put their dreams in a little box and say, "Yes, I've got dreams, of course, I've got dreams." Then they put the box away and bring it out once in a while to look in it, and yep, they're still there. These are great dreams, but they never even get out of the box. It takes an uncommon amount of guts to put your dreams on the line, to hold them up and say, "How good or how bad am I?" That's where courage comes in.

Erma Bombeck

Imagine the Possibilities
by Lesley Riley
PHOTO BY LES GAINS

CHAPTER 7
Teach Your Craft

Juggling teaching and motherhood

By Lesley Riley, quilter and mixed-media artist

When I started teaching, I had four children under the age of thirteen at home. Leaving town for three to five days not only meant that my husband had to take charge of the children and household, but it also doubled his workload in the small business we ran together. I learned how to juggle motherhood, marriage, our business and my career as an artist and teacher by moving slowly but surely in the direction of my dreams.

The first year, I taught at one out-of-town event; two in the second year; three the third year. The time in between was spent getting my name in print and working on my Web site. Showing my work, building a reputation and a following led to more requests to teach and enabled me to fill my classes.

By the time my children were older, my husband was used to running the family and business without me, and I was traveling and teach-

ing up to a dozen times a year—the amount that works for me.

My art and teaching has opened the door to many opportunities. Being able to take advantage of them without throwing my personal life out of balance is the result of carefully laying the groundwork and building the support at home that enables me to spread my wings and fly— both literally and figuratively.

I teach because I want to share what I have discovered. I found art late in life (age 40), and I often think about how sad my life would be without it. The process of making art gives purpose and meaning to my life. It's what I do for me. I want to spread the word to as many others as I can, so I teach.

It may look like I'm teaching techniques or fun projects, but what I'm really doing is showing my students how it feels to play, to create, to feed their soul. The secret is not what you make, but that you make it. Robert Henri sums it up best: "The object isn't to make art, it's to be in that wonderful state that makes art inevitable."

Weigh the pros and cons

People (more than ever!) are ready, willing, and eager to learn new crafts. This is a multibillion-dollar industry, and there isn't only room, but also a huge demand for more classes, supplies and books to satisfy its hungry audience. They'll learn a little and then want more, more, more!

Teaching craft classes is a very profitable way to make money with your art. Many artists start teaching classes, teaching leads to magazine articles and then sales of your art to gift shops, galleries and museums across the United States. Some people sell their work first, gain a wide audience and then start teaching. I started at home parties, moved on to larger audiences and then to selling my work.

There are several things to consider when you think you may want to teach classes. Everyone takes classes for very different reasons. Some want to talk and enjoy camaraderie, and some want to concentrate and learn. Often, other teachers want to take a class to gain new ideas and skills for their own classes. There are also multiple skill levels in each class—from the beginner to the more advanced student. And some people are just along because they are staying with a friend for the week and the friend had already signed up for classes but they don't really do any type of artwork, and on and on.

A large number of students take classes just to have an audience—they need their creative egos stroked. Add to the mix the fact that a lot of people are sensitive to products like bleach or solvent-based stamp cleaners. All of these things are perfectly normal, acceptable, and can complicate the hell out of your job as teacher. Before you get started down this crafty lane, ask yourself several questions:

• Am I generous? With my time, my ideas, my thoughts, my nurturing, my materials?
• What do I want to teach and how do I keep coming up with new class projects all the time?
• Do I want to spend a lot of time traveling or should I take only jobs that are close to home?
• Will this job take too much time from my family?
• Am I organized?
• Can I put together well-written instructions for class projects?
• Am I good at verbal communication?

Like any job, teaching has its pros and cons. Here's Lesley Riley's list:

Upside to teaching: traveling, getting away from home, meeting new people, seeing new places, sharing what you do, being admired, having groupies, encouraging others, finding your "tribe," getting paid for something you love to do, enjoying five minutes of fame, being in demand, being proud of what you do, having opportunities come your way, hanging out with artsy people, being an expert in your field and watching people's faces light up.

Downside to teaching: traveling, getting away from home, forgetting names, losing luggage, missing connections, having overweight luggage, shipping supplies, keeping accurate supply lists, buying expensive hotel food, teaching in cramped classrooms, feeling inadequate, not filling classes, experiencing stage fright, being exhausted, having sore feet, missing home and staying organized…always.

Find teaching venues

Places to teach your art and craft are many and varied: community colleges, craft stores, craft conventions, at home and online with e-classes to name a few. My primary experiences have been teaching in stamp stores and at rubber-stamp and art conventions. I asked different store owners about teaching in their stores. They all want sample boards, they want you to use what they carry and most are very eager to talk to you.

Be prepared

The importance of sample boards can't be stressed enough. Sample boards are a presentation of what you plan on teaching in your class. They are what sell your class, so make them interesting. Show items that will be made in class. It's a big no-no to make a fabulous sample and then change curriculum after the classes have been sold. It does happen, and in this way: A teacher sends captivating art as samples with her application to teach, the classes are sold and then she attempts to make her art into a class project. She finds out that she doesn't have the time or materials needed or can't reproduce the sample in a full classroom. So, she makes the class a little less than promised. You can imagine that people get cranky if they pay for one class and have to take an altogether different class. This happens so often that promoters have started stating in their contracts, very clearly, that you must teach the class that you show as a sample.

Along with your class sample boards, you must also provide a class description and prices for the store's newsletter. Most stores book classes on a quarterly basis, so you need to get the description to them three or four months before your class. Conventions are usually put together six months in advance, so they request all samples, proposals and applications even earlier. Getting your class onto the store's Web sites and newsletters and class schedules is how people will know what you're teaching. It also gives people a chance to save the date and sign up early. The faster you get all of your information out, the better chance you have of filling a classroom.

You must also provide a list of materials used in class. Get this to the store owner as soon as possible but no later than one month before class. The owner needs enough time to bring in some supplies that she may not have on hand so she can sell them during your classes. People want to buy what they use in class. A missed sales opportunity is a bad thing for everyone. It's in your best interest to keep the students happy and to help keep the stores in business.

Another part of your prep work is to carry supplies to classes. You can't teach a great class if you run out of supplies. Stock supplies that may not be in the student's regular class kit. To save space, think about supplying students with mini versions of full-sized products. For instance, I need to carry stamp pads around for my students to use in class. You can pack six Cat's Eyes' ink pads in the space that one full-sized ink pad takes. That means that six students can work simultaneously instead of six people waiting to share one ink pad. It also means that you can bring a larger variety of colors to class.

When I started, I had twelve knives, twelve scissors, twelve mats and so on. Your own house will be stuffed to the corners if you stock twelve of every single craft supply that you use, and my house was becoming so. It's not unreasonable to ask each student to bring a regular craft kit and maybe one or two specialized items. For my classes, the regular kit includes a heat gun, scissors, glue stick, a black fine-point Sharpie, double-stick tape, a craft knife, a metal-edged ruler and a cutting mat. This short list will not be an inconvenience for most crafters. But asking them to lug truckloads of art supplies to class is just cruel.

You can ask the store owner or the promoter if they will provide scratch paper, name tags, power strips and extension cords (if needed), paper towels and water for cleanup. Many realize that teachers have to fly to get to classes and don't have a lot of room in their luggage or a lot of money to ship these items, so they graciously try to accommodate. If they don't generally provide this in their classrooms, then it's up to you to bring these items.

Mailbox Display
by Carol Ramsey
PHOTO BY CAROL RAMSEY

Approaching store owners

By Carol Ramsey, owner of Stampotique

If you want to teach, bring in the stuff and show me. I expect that the work will be very professional; that it will be finished nicely and neatly; that it's an interesting technique, which the public will find fascinating and that the project will use products I already have on my shelves. It's also very important to me that the instructor has a pleasant attitude and maybe some prior teaching experience (not always). My belief has always been that people come to classes not only for the techniques, but also for the camaraderie and they seek a certain comfort level. I expect they will find all that and more when attending classes in our shop. They're paying hard-earned money and expect to get their money's worth. I intend that they will.

Our teachers can, and have, made good money, so it's definitely in their best interest to come up with great ideas for classes and set the class fee at reasonable rates so that lots of students sign up! I do remind them that rubber-stamping is a craft and not fine art. Let's have fun!

Remember, you're trying to make your students as comfortable as possible.

When preparing for a class, the balancing act is in making a class project that's cool enough to capture a student's attention and excites them enough to sign up, while also developing a project that can be completed during a certain time frame. People want the most for their buck, naturally! But, how can you make it so without being deceptive about how long a project will actually take them to complete in real time?

Obviously, you have to take time to construct the project, writing the steps as you go. Once you have it all figured out, hone it so that you know approximately how long it will take an average student to complete. Keep in mind that you're taking up some of their class time giving instructions. If you need to do some of the steps ahead of time, such as cutting paper to size, then so be it. Sometimes you'll have to cut book board or cardstock and put it in the class packet. You may even need to pre-stamp some cards if you don't have enough stamps to go around. To save time, you can insert into the class kits needles, cord, fibers, and other items that will take too long for each student to cut. That's part of the prep work. It's part of your job.

People often have several demands on their time outside of the classroom; the class time is their only craft time and they want to finish a project in class. That's the goal and, by golly, you'd better have a project that fits that bill. If you design a project that takes more time to complete than allotted for class, tell the students in the class description. That way, they know what they are getting ahead of time.

People can be sensitive to many products. If you use irritants in class, such as bleach, say so in your class description so people can make an informed decision about whether or not to sign up for the class. Any fumigant sprays, even hairspray, should be used outside of the classroom. If your classroom is in a store, be sensitive to other shoppers and personnel who aren't taking the class. You can generally step just outside the front or back door to spread the fumes.

After you've got your project down pat and you've shipped the sample boards and the all the class information to the store, it's time to write up step-by-step instructions and get those class packets together. A lot of teachers I know don't hand out instructions in class, so I suppose it's not necessary. But, I think people should not have to try to listen and watch you demo a project while taking notes. I hand out instructions because no one can remember every little step of each project, especially after a long weekend of taking five classes. There is a study that shows that, when you're teaching, people can remember

Keys to a successful recreational experience
By Judi Watanabe, founder of rubber-stamp manufacturer JudiKins, Inc.

1. Anticipation: *Get participants excited about the event. A good write up with a clear but interesting description is a must. Be sure to explain what is expected of the students.*

2. Preparation: *This benefits both you and the students. Make sure you have your ducks in a row. Gather supplies, plan activities and make lists. For teaching craft or art classes, think about what tools you need and the steps needed to make a project. Don't forget to give your students a list of what to bring. (They need to prepare as well.)*

3. Participation: *When teaching the class it needs to be more than just a lesson, make it an event to remember. It's important that students leave feeling a sense of accomplishment. Give clear instructions and watch for confusion. If you see potential problems, offer positive and constructive advice. If you can, fix their disasters.*

4. Recollection: *Make sure the students leave with something and that you review and evaluate the event. What works? What needs improvement? Give participants an instructor evaluation form to fill out. Let them know how important it is for you to continually improve your classes. Encourage them to be honest, and if they are more comfortable being anonymous, let them be.*

Choosing your subject matter

By Lisa Renner, polymer-clay, mixed-media and paper-arts artist

When I create a new class, I first try to imagine the kinds of classes that I personally like to take, then I work it out from there. For example, I enjoy learning new techniques. Even better, but not crucial, is if there is a project involved. If I am teaching at a store, I ask the owner what the customers prefer. I have taught for stores that cater to customers who are more technique focused and don't care about a finished project. Others are definitely project oriented, so in those cases my class will be designed so that students take home a completed project. I try to work with the store owners, harmoniously combining what I like to teach with what most interests the customers of that particular store.

For those considering teaching: Don't be afraid to submit your ideas to store owners. Be prepared to discuss potential changes that might better serve the store and its customers as long as you're still able to stay true to your art. And one important thing to remember: Not everyone likes everything. Some ideas are better accepted than others—don't get discouraged. Just keep creating. It's not always easy, but if we can take constructive criticism and put it to good use, it can benefit us in our growth as artists and as teachers.

Mokume Gane Pendant
by Lisa Renner
PHOTO BY LES GAINS

and process only about 40 percent of what you say. So, make it as easy for your students as you can.

You're charging for your classes, and the least you can do is type instructions with color copies of the sample boards included. If you think the copies are too expensive, consider that one dollar of the class fee is going to pay for them. Is that too high a price for student appreciation?

Brainstorm for classes

When you're developing your classes, be flexible, stay ahead of trends, but also develop a sixth sense about when to stay the course even if a technique seems to become overburdened. I stopped doing altered journals as soon as I realized that everyone around me seemed to be making pages. What a mistake! Instead of being a trendsetter in the field, I played myself right out of it by trying to stay one step ahead.

There are people who will want to brainstorm with you, and at first you'll be pleased that you have someone to talk art with. You may then find that their classes just happen to be the ones you helped them come up with. Also, your friend may feel that it's your classes that she came up with. So, to avoid any hard feelings, brainstorming classes should probably be a solitary task.

My storm starts by going through all my supplies and gewgaw drawers. Sometimes I see a product that I haven't used in a long time and it sparks an idea. Or I see that I have a lot of binder clips that I've been planning on using in class "someday." This may be just the day!

In designing your classes, offer the unexpected. Everyone loves nice surprises. The unexpected can be as simple as an extra bit of pretty fiber or charms tucked into the class packet, door prizes, or even a dish of candy. Your students are special in your life and integral to your chosen profession. Make them feel that way.

Preparing for class

By Sylvia Luna, collage and altered-book artist

When I teach a class, it's the easy ending to a long, obsessively planned subject. I begin the process long before the class meets to make a time-consuming project. I don't work quickly so all that I make develops over time, some faster than others. First, I sit and create with items I have collected. I then either keep the finished project as a class sample (depending on whether I have the supplies used in quantity), submit it for publication or decide to sell it. From start to finish, I never exactly know what will transform before me.

Once it's finished and I feel it would be a great convention class, I backtrack through my first steps by creating it again mentally, then I record all the steps and supplies used. From there, I write a rough draft for the students, as well as teacher notes for myself. Last, but not least, I make a list of supplies to share and supplies given. When I travel out of state, I also make lists of which box contains which supplies. "The Golden Rule" helps me decide what to provide for each student—I imagine I am the one paying for the class. Generosity has never been a regret of mine.

Artist Trading Card
by Sylvia Luna
PHOTO BY LES GAINS

Calm your nerves

Performance anxiety is a problem in all aspects of being your own company. But it's especially noticeable when you have to show a demo or promote yourself so that you become more recognized. Speaking in front of a crowd, ughhh…if I could do classes with a bag over my head, I would. I don't like people looking at me, period. Hmmmm…am I in the wrong business? No, because I know that I have a lot of experience and knowledge to share. I've taken so many classes from art killers that I'm determined that my students learn to feel free in their creating.

If you want to teach classes, start by taking classes! It's an entirely different feeling to sit in the class rather than be the head of it. Performance anxiety runs rampant in classes on both sides. It may help you to know that your students have as much anxiety as you do. When you step outside of yourself and help them relax and overcome their fears, it automatically helps you master your own.

When you take an art class, listen carefully to student questions. Watch their response at the answers and listen to the side conversations among the students. Are they about the class, teacher, materials or lack thereof? Are they getting what they wanted out of the class? All of this will help you improve your own classes. You'll be less anxious about your performance if you're prepared with great classes.

Get it in writing

A long time ago, when I started teaching rubber-stamp classes, there was still a small community feel to the craft. Everybody knew everybody, and a handshake was all that was needed to make an agreement. Now, however, there are so many more stores, companies and personalities involved that a formal agreement is probably the best way to go. I say "probably" because if you already know the person and have had several successful interactions with them in the past, then the status quo is fine. Anything else just seems rude. But if you don't know

Sandra McCall
P.O. Box 351, Dewey, AZ 86327
(999) 999-9999
mccallss@arthouse.com
www.arthouse525.com

Workshop Agreement

Thank you for your interest in hosting my workshops at your store. I am excited to come and show your customers new and creative ways to use rubber stamps and related supplies.

Store _____   Contact _____
Name _____   Phone _____
Address _____   E-mail _____

I have you scheduled for the following classes and/or demonstrations:

Class	Date	Time	Fee
_____	_____	_____	$__.__/student
_____	_____	_____	$__.__/student
_____	_____	_____	$__.__/student
_____	_____	_____	$__.__/student
_____	_____	_____	$__.__/student

Optional: demonstration

_____   _____   _____ @ $75.00 per hour

A minimum of six students per class is required. The maximum is as many students as your store can comfortably hold. Out-of-area stores require a minimum booking of 5 classes. Class fees are due upon completion of final class. Demonstrations are available in conjunction with classes at a fee of $75 per hour. Class sample boards will be shipped to you at least 45 days prior to scheduled workshops.

I will call 2 days before I have to leave for your store to get a head count for each class. You must guarantee this student count. A class packet will be left for "no-shows" in exchange for their class fee. I will prep a few extra packets for late sign-ups.

Everyone who takes a class, sits in on a class, or observes a class pays the full class fee.

Transportation, hotel close to teaching facility, and meals are to be arranged and covered by your store. For out-of-area stores, airline flights will be booked 45 days prior to class dates. A $100.00 cancellation fee is required after airline booking.
There is an automobile mileage fee of $0.25. It is my understanding that transportation will be:

_____
(Airline flight, automobile, etc.)

A supply list showing stamps, supplies, and accessories used in the workshop accompanies this agreement. This is provided to you as a courtesy, so that you may arrange to have the stock on hand for customers to purchase, but it is a long list and it is understood that you may choose not to bring in everything listed. I will do my part in directing students to alternate stamps and supplies (for purchase) that you may already have on hand.

Students need to bring any materials specified in the class descriptions to class; I will provide all other project materials.

Store Representative _____   Date _____

Please sign and return agreement via e-mail or post mail as soon as possible. Thank you!

the second party, then draw up a contract for both of you to sign!

A couple of years ago, I had scheduled classes with a store in Albuquerque when a store owner from El Paso (about four hours away) contacted me to see if I'd teach at her store. It would save her the trip expenses, as she would only have to pay for the four-hour trip. It would benefit me as well, because I was staying with a friend and could extend my visit for a week by sandwiching the two stores together. One weekend at one store, visit with my friend, and then another store of classes on the following weekend. I know that small stores are generally strapped for cash (as most of us are) so I'll work with them to save dollars if I can. I only had phone knowledge of the owner and she seemed nice enough, so I said OK.

While teaching, I was honored that she would take time from her busy schedule to participate in a couple of my classes. So I may have accidentally broken one of my teaching rules—I catered to her just a teeny bit more than the other students. You know what happens when you break your own rules, right? It's not pretty.

So, after all classes were wrapped, I handed her a student count for each class as I customarily do. She pouted and said, "You mean I have to pay for my classes?" I calmly said "yes," and the atmosphere turned brutal.

What did I learn from this? In hindsight, I realized that we were both wrong. We both made assumptions, assumptions that could have been made plain if I'd drawn up a contract and stuck to it. Will I teach at her store again? Heck no! If she calls, I'm booked until the year 2098. Do I think that she'll ever deal with me again? Nope.

So, where's the balance? I only have my ideas and kits with instructions to sell. Where do you draw the line in giving them away? People who expect me to give them classes because I'm teaching at their venue insult me. As far as I am concerned, the benefit to them is that I'm selling their goods by demonstrating them and letting students use them in class. It's a fact that people want to buy what they have just enjoyed using, so it's an easy sale, but a sale nonetheless. I'm also bringing people into the store who will come back to make more purchases based on what they learned that day. The stores where I teach get a line at the register from my classes, and that completes my job. You make your own policies, but "free classes" is a subject that comes up often. You may want to spell out your ideas on this in your contract.

So learn, once again, from my mistakes. Once something awful comes between two people, it rarely can be repaired. Good and honorable words can be exchanged, but you can't take back the initial sting. Make a contract and stick to it! (And don't cater to one student more than another, even if you really, really want to.)

You can see my contract for teaching at rubber-stamp stores on page 61. If I've known the organizer for a while, I don't bother with the official agreement because we already have an informal agreement. If I'm not busy the next time they want to have classes, then that means the verbal agreements are working out just fine for us. But I've learned to show new people my standard contract so we can proceed to negotiate from there. Feel free to use my contract as a template, changing it as needed.

Sell yourself

You need to sell your classes. You're a big part of them, so sell yourself, too! Part of your image is developing your teaching style. Hand out critiques. Ask students what they liked and didn't like about the class and how you could have made it better?

I once handed out critiques to students attending a convention and taking classes in Florida. The questionnaire asked if the students enjoyed themselves, if they got what they were looking for from class, would they change anything about the class and things like that. Then it came to this question: "What would you have done differently?" A student replied that she would have worn black to class. It made me laugh, but it also taught me a lesson. Each person is the star in his or her own life. Everything is all about her—not my classes and not me.

You must stay current. You're the expert and people look to you for guidance. This is actually harder than you may think. It's time consuming to learn as much as you can about products, but it makes you a better teacher and salesperson. Keep your eyes and ears open. Go to craft and hobby shows. Read about art and crafts. Watch craft shows. And listen, listen, listen.

Publish first

My aunt once told me that I'm foolish to teach what I sell, because it's the same as giving it away. I can see her point, but I enjoy teaching much more than mass production. I prefer to share my ideas and let someone else build off of them. I enjoy the interaction with my students. I learn as much from them as they learn from me, so it's a good fit for me.

But, a word of caution, if you have what you think is the last great idea for a new technique; try to get it published before you teach a class. That way, the original idea is more likely attributed to you. Once you teach anything, it spreads among people like wildfire by word of mouth, in chat rooms, discussion boards, more magazines, television and so on. You tune in to DIY Network one day and see someone else teaching a duplicate of the bracelet you taught in class. It's so identical that you wonder if it *is* the bracelet he made in your class. Your name isn't mentioned, and you're angry. However, if you've already published the piece, someone knows the truth. That should give you a little piece of mind.

The joys of teaching

Michael Jacobs, sculptural-book, wood-craft and leather-craft artist

In 1990, when I owned Dimensional Graphics in Seattle, I received a commission to design and build the Kodak Goodwill Games World's Largest Photo Album. This was a truly life-altering experience. I worked on this project over a nine-month period with much down time while I waited for photos to be delivered and various inspections by Kodak officials. The completed components for this monster album sat in my studio for quite awhile before I could complete the final assembly process. As I looked at the huge covers, the steel-reinforced spine section and the 184 laminated pages day after day, I started to think of books as sculptures, composed of separate parts. I'd been making 3-D craft and sculptural objects since I was a kid, but approaching books as sculpture was a whole new ball game for me. I bought books on bookbinding, experimented wildly and got very excited as I contemplated pursuing book arts as my next career. I'd always wanted to teach and decided I'd create and teach paper-craft and book-art workshops.

I closed down my studio and started teaching in 1993 and have never looked back. Teaching workshops is second only to my love of designing and making mixed-media sculptures, books and other objects.

My goal in 1993 was to teach part time so I would have plenty of time to explore art and craft. My biggest surprise, especially since I'm efficient and well organized by nature, was that teaching consumed way more time than I ever thought it would! Developing new workshops, preparing handouts and samples for each workshop, getting contracts signed, booking tickets, packing and travelling, then unpacking and decompressing—it all takes a huge amount of time. And teaching requires all of this!

On the other hand, the act of teaching is extremely rewarding for me in many ways. I thrive on designing new workshop projects, sharing my knowledge and expertise with others, interacting with my students and seeing the obvious joy on their faces when they create something they're proud of, or when they explore a new and, perhaps, uncomfortable area or technique and get over the fear of not doing it right. The act of teaching is always challenging, interesting and downright fun! On top of all that, I enjoy hanging out with my students and other instructors and have made friends in many states. The name recognition I attained as a result of teaching led to how-to books, television appearances, articles and DVDs.

Another wonderful surprise about teaching is that I sometimes have time to see the sights in the cities I visit. I've seen wild alligators on Sanibel Island in Florida, gotten close enough to touch large-scale and breathtaking ice sculptures at the International Ice Carving Championship in Anchorage, Alaska, viewed an open volume of the Gutenberg Bible in Austin, Texas, and toured the Rock and Roll Hall of Fame and Museum in Cleveland, Ohio, among dozens of other experiences way too numerous to mention.

My advice to new teachers is to plan carefully how much material or how many projects can be taught in the time allotted, rehearse the workshop thoroughly, limit the students to a number that can be handled comfortably, prepare components for each step if appropriate, and demo techniques at the beginning of class or as needed on individual projects, which allows the students to focus on the creative aspects of the projects and not stress out over the how-it's-done part! Good communication skills, an open and friendly attitude, the ability to stay on track and well-constructed samples are musts. I strongly believe in teaching original projects. To me, it's not ethical to take a class with projects designed by the instructor, and then teach them without the instructor's permission.

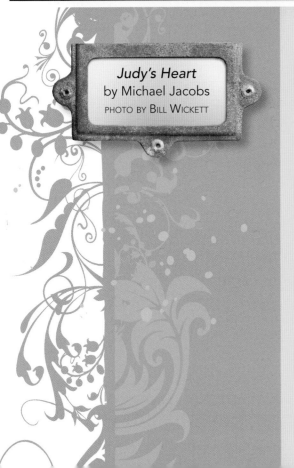

Judy's Heart
by Michael Jacobs
PHOTO BY BILL WICKETT

Fields
by Sherrill Kahn
PHOTO BY SHERRILL KAHN

CHAPTER 8
Be a Writer

From artist to author

By Sherrill Kahn, rubber-stamp designer and founder of rubber-stamp company Impress Me

I love to teach. It was my career choice and I taught for thirty years in the public schools. After retiring, my husband Joel and I started a small rubber-stamp company called Impress Me, which caused a lot of wonderful things to happen.

About ten years ago, Teesha Moore asked me to teach and sell at Artfest in Bellevue, Washington. We had just started our rubber-stamp company. The sales at the show were phenomenal and have been ever since. I have only done three shows where I sold the stamps, but all were very successful. Joel and I decided that selling at shows was not our thing, so now we sell internationally from our Web site.

While I was at Artfest, Teesha introduced me to Sharilyn Miller, the editor of Somerset Studio. She asked me to show her some of my work, and I started writing articles for her. Writing for Somerset Studio led to my being asked to write my first book. I feel that writing articles is the best way to get people familiar with your work.

It also seems to open other doors. Writing my first book led to getting a paint line and a Travel Paint Studio with Jacquard, several fabric lines with Robert Kaufman, products with Clearsnap, working with Janome sewing machines, and now recently an association with Walnut Hollow.

I have been teaching internationally for the last ten years, and I have met wonderful people who have inspired me to push the envelope with my own work. Because of the first article for Somerset Studio, I have three books now and write for many magazines. I encourage everyone to submit his work for publication in magazines. If you have enough work for a book, contact a publisher and create a proposal.

I think the best advice I could give is to just "do it." I have been rejected a lot of times and just thanked the publisher for their time and re-submitted new ideas. We all have fears, but try-ing again with new ideas for publication pushes us to be even better. If I hadn't written that first article for Somerset Studio, my life would be very different. I wish you all the best in your cre-ative pursuits.

There are very few of us artsy types who are able to support ourselves with only one kind of work. Most of us do or have done practically everything described in this book. One handcrafted item often requires hours and hours—maybe even days or weeks of labor. If this is so with your craft and you are already working as many hours as you can, then it may be wise to find a way to cut your labor and still generate income. Writing how-to books and articles is a perfect way to do this. It will also give you higher visibility and keep you at the forefront of the pack. Visibility is all part of the game and writing can get you that much-sought-after "expert" status. I know—I can feel you thinking that maybe the word "expert" is too strong. Well, think of it this way: You know what you know, and that is what you will write about. Continually learning, talking and writing about your art is what makes you an expert. Embrace it and enjoy the glow. When you are deemed an expert, your art and craft will be in higher demand. In other words, it ups the value of your work; you can raise your prices and take a vacation now and then. The other plus is that you can promote your sites, your other books and yourself with little blurbs at the end of your articles.

Writing outlets

Even if you don't consider yourself a writer, there are several options that don't require a literary degree. Well, it's nowhere near a necessity, actually. In fact, for how-to articles, plain speak is the way to go.

What is very important, however, is having access to a computer. You need a computer. Gone are the days of typing a huge manuscript and rushing it off to your editor through snail mail. Editors will often require you to send JPEGs or TIFFs of photos and text files of your docu-

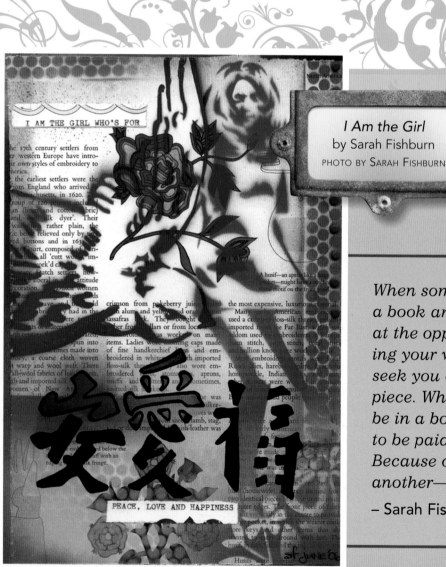

I Am the Girl
by Sarah Fishburn
PHOTO BY SARAH FISHBURN

When someone asks you to be in a book and offers to pay you, leap at the opportunity. People love seeing your work in books and may seek you out to buy an original art piece. When someone invites you to be in a book and there's no chance to be paid, leap at the opportunity. Because often one thing leads to another—you just never know!

– Sarah Fishburn, *collage artist*

ments so that they can stick your disk into their computer and start working right away. If this sounds like nonsensical jargon to you, get a book and a computer and get busy learning.

Art and craft magazines are always looking for contributions to their pages. You are half the reason they exist, so don't be afraid to approach them. Just about any magazine that you open will have submission guidelines printed somewhere in those glossy pages. You don't have to go out and buy every single craft magazine. Most of them have the information on their Web sites as well. Follow the guidelines and you are practically a shoe-in. Most of them will even say in the guidelines. "You do not have to worry about the writing—we will help you." They just want great new ideas and samples that their readers will love.

Do familiarize yourself with each periodical, either with pages in hand or through their Web sites. The secret to success is to match your art or craft to their publication. If the title of the magazine is *Cloth Paper Scissors*, then you know you should probably have some cloth and some paper in the project. Your metal and glass humanoid figures will most certainly be rejected even if they are the coolest things around town.

If your idea does get the old rejection boot, you have two ways to go. You can either drop it altogether or submit it to another publication. Wait for the yay or nay, though. Multiple submissions at the same time are heavily frowned upon in the publishing world. You don't want to get blacklisted before you even start.

Along this vein are zines, e-zines, booklets, newsletters, and even greeting cards. The pay scale varies, with magazines paying the most—generally around $50 per article. It's truthfully very little, but if you are a prolific writer, and you have a computer, then you can create quite a little profit for yourself. A copy of the *Writer's Market* (F+W Publications) will further aid in your search of writing outlets.

Books

Writing books will possibly get you more money, but it's also more work to write and sell a book. You may need no writing experience for craft magazines, but it's different with a book. There is a lot more information, many chapters to write, and many more projects to design. It's possible that each project requires multiple steps for the instructions. This requires not only the ability to write and produce cool crafts, but also the ability to organize a mountain of paper, projects and computer files. You also need to be able to do research and to enjoy it.

So, yes, yes, yes. You love all of the work and eagerly look forward to seeing your book proudly perched next to your favorite authors in the bookstores. You've got a fantastic idea for a book—it's practically all written. How do you get your book to the right acquisitions editor?

Well, there is more homework involved. The *Writer's Market* (F+W Publications) can get you to the gatekeeper, but it will take a phone call to see who the current acquisitions editor is. After many years of writing books, I have found that editors come and go faster than…well, I don't know what, but they do. So, call and at least have the correct name on your query letter.

Your first query letter should be somewhat formal. That is to say that you need to follow guidelines. After you get to know your editor, you can be informal or funny in your pitches, but with your first book…well, let's just say now's not the time. So, get with the program and learn to write a good query letter. This is your first chance to make an impression—try to make it nothing less than fantastic.

A word of caution—even after your editor tells you that you can submit a casual e-mail proposal, keep it on the semiformal side. I have submitted letters only to find that they had been turned over to someone in another department or to a new editor—someone I did not previously know. This can be embarrassing. You would not use the same tone with someone that you have worked with as you would with a stranger. It's possible that the new person will not think you are as funny as you think you are. They are not already as fond of you as your previous editor may have been, so keep it professional. Also, in your correspondence, never *ever* blast anyone or any book to an editor. Like all businesses, the publishing world is incestuous; everyone knows everyone, so keep it cool.

To find out how to get published, I bought the second edition of *The Complete Idiot's Guide to Getting Published* (Alpha). I followed the advice to a T, and it worked! The authors did say to be prepared for a long wait that could be followed by rejection letters. Perhaps I was lucky in that I was at the right place at the right time, but I got e-mail notice back within a week of my mailing. They loved the letter and wanted to see more in the form of an official proposal.

Basically, there are two steps to submitting your work to a publisher. The first is the query letter, a one-page letter of introduction. You write a paragraph that describes your book, a paragraph that describes the market for your book and a paragraph devoted to the description of you.

The second step is the proposal. It includes a table of contents, a book outline, sample artwork (possibly slides—it depends on the publisher), and an excerpt from one of the chapters. If your query letter is well received, the acquisitions editor lets you know exactly what they need next. But, do your homework and learn as much as you can about this process. When you step into the world of book publishing, you enter the way-too-busy business sector. Don't expect to be led around by the hand, while you mumble, "Well, I'm just a beginner, I don't really know what I'm doing…."

Query letters

Be positive, professional and to the point in your query. To begin writing it, start with yourself—that should be the easiest subject. Let your mind spill everything you can think of that relates to you as the author, including your

> *The first piece I sent in to a magazine was rejected and I also didn't get accepted to teach at the first two art conventions I applied for. But that didn't stop me.*
>
> — **Traci Bautista,** *handmade-book and mixed-media collage artist*

platform. A platform is your past experiences as a writer, a speaker or a teacher. The publishers want to know how much of a following you have. Higher visibility means higher sales for your book.

After you have written your life story, take those ten pages and condense them into one paragraph that introduces you to the editor. Don't toss anything though. You'll need longer bios and self-portraits after your book sells and people are curious about you.

Now that you are warmed up, you can move on to the book. To keep it short, explain what your book is about, how it differs from other books on the market, and how it will benefit readers (making them want to buy it).

The marketing section covers demographics. Who and how many people will buy this book?

The last paragraph should be a thank you for the time of the reader.

If this is an unsolicited query, include a self-addressed, stamped envelope so that the editor can reply quickly and with little trouble, otherwise you may hear nothing back at all. Some editors accept e-mail queries, while others do not like them, so check to be sure. E-mail may mean a faster response for you.

Proposals

When broken down, the layers of a proposal are not all that difficult to write. Again, keep it easy to read, but now is the time to turn up the glow factor. You need to hit on these key elements: A cover page, the pitch, a proposed table of contents, and a sample chapter (or an excerpt). With art or crafts, you may also be asked to send the physical work, photos, or slides with your proposal.

The cover page should hold the proposed title, your name, your address, your telephone number, and your e-mail address.

The pitch is where you sell your book. You get to convince the publishers that this book will sell and sell big! What is your book about? Who will buy this book? Is there a large market screaming to get their hands on

your book? Go back to your files and dig out the massive amounts of info that you tossed from your query letter. You can use a lot of it here.

Check out your competition—list their books, describe their success or weakness and how your book will be an even bigger seller. Remember, though, no cutting. Your editor may very well have edited one of those books!

Write a paragraph about how this book can be marketed. Are you a friend of Oprah's and can gain instant access to several news and variety shows? Do you already have a huge following of fans that will guarantee that they and millions of their friends will rush out to buy your book? Hint: If you are a nationally and internationally known teacher, then you have a large following. Even if you are somewhat reclusive, you *do* have a large following. If you've kept up with your e-mail lists, you have access to them and, potentially, all their friends as well.

If you have solid acquaintances who are also well known in your chosen field or are famous stars in their own right, and they will contribute to your book, then let it be known. Oprah will write the foreword for your book? Spill it baby! You're in!

Pitch yourself as well. List your credentials, any previous publishing experience, awards, and accomplishments. Let the publisher know that you are uniquely qualified to write and hype this book. Show that you can and will sell this book!

Next is your table of contents. Include the chapter titles and a short summary of each chapter.

A sample chapter will show your writing style. Make it one that represents your voice.

You may opt to send recent publicity, reviews or articles concerning you and your work. If it's good, include it!

Your first proposal will be the most involved. After your first book, you will have earned trust that you can deliver, so it will be a lot more casual.

In both the query and the proposal, write it, read it, re-read it, and cut out extra words. It's that simple, or is it? Even if you think you are not struggling with your letter, look through books that have samples of query letters. Log on to the Internet and key in the search words "query letters." You can read queries and pitches written by professionals—many of them ex-agents or editors who know what they are talking about. Take their advice. It's ready and just waiting for you.

Publishers

Get a copy of the *Writer's Market* (F+W Publications)—the most recent one that you can. It's unbelievably packed with information. Start by working your way through that. You can get an idea of submission guidelines, type of work accepted and even pay scales. Use a highlighter to mark the places that you might like to contact.

Go to your bookstore and walk the aisles. Whose books do you admire? Who publishes the type of book that you want to write? Where do you fit in?

After you find a publisher, submit your work and wait. It may take a while. Resist the urge to make phone calls to see if your contract is on the way. If you've included a self-addressed stamped envelope and you still hear nothing after six months, it's realistic to expect that your query letter may have hit the round file. Either come up with a new idea or go down your list and submit to the next publisher, but do not submit the same idea to multiple houses simultaneously!

Contracts

Yay! The big day is here—your contract finally arrives! And it's long and full of strange words.

I have read, repeatedly, that you should hire an attorney to look publishing contracts over, and you probably should. I don't. I only deal with reputable people so I'm not afraid that what they are doing is not on the up and up. But, Sandra, you ask, isn't that like burying your head in the sand? Yeah, it is. I already told you that I don't like to think about anything that has to do with grown-up business stuff.

Here is my logic in this. (I do know I'll get a lot of negative response here, so I will state again that this is how I do business and you should certainly conduct your business in a way that makes you comfortable.) My path is to read the contract and highlight anything I do not understand. Then I ask my editor or contract manager to explain what they are trying to say. The very words "publishing contracts" sound scary because you are usually dealing with a corporation of some type, and you know that a contract is binding. So, of course, you should enter into the deal with as clear a picture as you can. But contracts are not all that difficult to read.

If you sit down in a calm manner with a glass of tea or soda or a cup of coffee (caffeine is highly recommended for reading contracts as all those long words are a bore) and start reading, you will see that you can, indeed, understand it. For those ridiculously long words, have a dictionary on hand before you start reading. True, they throw in way too many words in an effort to cover every-

thing, including their, ummm…derriere. But, it's to cover yours as well. A publishing house will have standard contracts that they use with all their authors. The money will be different and the deadlines, titles, and specifics will vary from author to author, but basically, the contracts are all the same. A publishing house will not want to write a deceptive contract and ruin their reputation, so you do not have to worry too much about the big bad wolf. On the other hand, not understanding what you sign can lead to feelings of unfairness, victimization and publishing house duplicity. So, if you read the contract, do not understand it and don't trust your publishing house or editor, then by all means, hire an attorney to check it out for you.

One surprising aspect of the contract is that the author does not have much, if anything at all, to do with the cover art or the title. Publishing houses have been in the business of selling books for many years and they have a lot of money riding on each new book, so they tend to trust their marketing team and in-house artists to decide what will sell much more than they trust you. Even though I hate that loss of creative control, they may have a point there. They can also print and reprint your book or excerpts in just about any manner they choose. Sometimes they choose to make a book smaller than you envisioned and print it on a paper you don't like. So, yeah, you may find some surprise in the finished product. Expect and accept that, and you will be a happy camper.

Blogs

The other thing that I found shocking when I wrote my first book, is that *you* have to promote your book. I envisioned myself leading a jet-setting glamorous life where the publishing house paid my way to go to all these different book signings that they set up. Well, unless you are at the top of *The New York Times* bestseller list every week, then that just isn't so. You are in charge of hyping your own book, and if you do a good job, it will sell well, and you may get the chance to write another book. That's the real world.

No matter how insightful or groundbreaking your book is, no one will ever know if you don't advertise. Well, you want to get your books noticed too, so blog it up baby! You can put your books and several sample pages onto your Web site. On Web sites, talk up the book and then put a link directly to the site where they can purchase the book. If you have no Web site, all of this can be posted on a blog as well. In fact, it's easier to upload pictures and a running stream of genius expression from you onto a blog than onto a Web site. The difference is that a Web site is much more structured so the learning curve is higher. I'm giving away free mini classes on my blogs with the goal of driving more customers that are interested to buy my books and DVDs. The free classes should be passed around the Internet much like word-of-mouth advertising. The other advantage of a blog is that it's free.

Forest Queen
by Roberta Altschuler
PHOTO BY ROBERTA ALTSCHULER

CHAPTER 9
Sell Your Art

Making money from your art

By Roberta Altschuler, beader, stamp designer and founder of rubber-stamp company ERA Graphics

A few of the things I have noticed on this path of "making money with my art" is that I never have enough inventory to take to a show. This means that, until recently, I stuck with stamp shows or mixed-media shows so that I would have something to sell when the bags were all gone.

In real estate, the mantra is location, location. In art, it's venue, venue. What sells at one show may not even rate a second glance at another. What brings sticker shock at one venue is considered a mere piffle at another. I have a strong style, and my work has a distinctive look. Only experience has taught me where my work sells and where it doesn't.

This is such a personal experience that determining the "best" venue is a matter of trial and error. As my husband says, if you can read the public taste and figure out when and where to be, you will be rich by Thursday.

That brings me to another observation—you rarely, if ever, get rich selling art. Of course, that does not deter scads of people from trying to make it each year. And it shouldn't deter you, as there is an amazing amount of satisfaction you can get by doing what you love. It would help if I didn't do something that takes sometimes hundreds of hours to complete, but here I'm doing piecework!

While you don't want creating art to be work, you still must apply some business sense so as not to lose money. Most of the business part of art is common sense. The biggest mistake a new artist makes is confusing income with profit. In other words, when you go to a show and come home with a pile of cash, you need to subtract all your expenses before you can say you made any money. This may sound obvious but I know tons of people who are dazzled by the cash and shocked to find out at the end of the year that they lost money.

Whatever you do, be fanatic about your technique. Do the very best job on each and every piece and make sure to finish it meticulously, even if it takes gobs more time and some do-overs. People may not know how to do what you do, but they sure can spot sloppy workmanship.

The best piece of advice I can give to new craft artists is to start small and slowly. Stay near home and find venues that marry well with what you do, so that you can minimize expenses (and get used to eating fast food). Listen to your customers— what they like and how much they are willing to pay for it. Check out the other vendors at a show, how they display their work and how they market themselves. Ask them what shows work best for them. Slowly move your circle of venues out and experiment with display ads in the various craft and art magazines. Always have business cards, postcards with professional pictures of your work, and an e-mail address. But most of all, develop a thick skin—some people talk to their friends right in front of you as though you are deaf—and they can be clueless. Remember, everyone is a critic, but very few can create good art.

Your product

I've repeatedly heard and read that to make great sales, you must make things that are functional. I couldn't disagree more. In my experience, functionality is a plus, but when people are looking for handcrafted items, they want something that moves them. You can move a person by stimulating any of their senses. If your booth or wares smell, sound, look or feel exciting to the potential buyer, then she'll stop and browse. Getting the buyer to stop and look is the first step to success. If it appeals to her sense of humor or intelligence, it has a greater chance at being a bestseller. If nostalgia or personalization is involved in your wares, that's even better.

Appealing to a person's vanity is also a good idea, such as selling jewelry or wearable art that makes them look or feel great. Oh! Don't forget the kids. Most people have a soft spot for their children and pets. So have something for them as well.

We live in a harried, hectic world. Today, one of the biggest benefits to a buyer is saving time. If you've figured out a great timesaver that also looks really cool, you're in!

Most craft and art buyers are looking for a gift, whether it's for themselves or someone else. As for functionality—well, he can find functionality at any big-box store. Even if your items are functional art, you'll make more sales by emphasizing the art, originality and superb craftsmanship over the function.

However, if you create something that's functional art, make sure that it's just that. If it's a vase, it must hold water, if it's wearable art, the person must be able to comfortably wear it. Make sure that your creation doesn't fall apart at the first use.

It's common wisdom to have a few smaller, less expensive items in your booth, too: $2 to $20 items work well for me. These are the items that people pick up, sometimes not even for gifts, but as personal souvenirs. Buyers at large destination conventions or craft fairs are often looking for reminders of their day as well. They want a little something to take home for themselves and their like-minded friends. So, you might want to think in the souvenir direction, too.

Making gifts that do double duty for the customer is also a good idea. I stock my booth with $12 greeting cards that are both gifts and cards. These offer time-saving and cost-effective benefits to my customers. It's simply a piece of neutral-colored cardstock folded to make a 5" x 7" (13cm x 18cm) card. Then I put a clean, rectangular piece of white card on the front. Onto that I print a variety of different sentiments. To save time myself, I use the color printer. Attached to the front of the card is a small handcrafted pin or pendant. This item has proven to be one of my bestsellers.

Because you're selling gifts, have some gift cards ready so the buyer can just pick up the whole package and go. It'll be a timesaver for her, thus an added benefit to her purchase. Unless handmade cards are your main focus, make them very simple and inexpensive. A white piece of cardstock, folded over and with three stripes of cheery color washed across the front works. Then print the sentiment inside the card.

I've noticed that people pick the cards with a sentiment on them over the blank cards. I used to sell cards in my craft booth in an art mart. I thought it would be more appealing to have blank cards so they would reach a wider audience. Buyers could write anything that pertained to their purposes for buying the card, I reasoned. I wondered why my cards weren't selling as well as expected; the cost was low enough, and they were very pretty. In this particular craft mall, we had to share time walking the floor, which is a very good place to learn a lot. I was a couple of feet from my stall when I overheard the ladies talking about my cards. They were actually picking them up, looking at them, admiring them, and then putting them back. One said to the other that she was looking for a birthday card and that she wished the cards had "Happy Birthday" printed on them. The other woman agreed that sentiments on them would be so much better. Well, there you go. People don't want to take the time to write in their own sentiments. Or maybe a blank card doesn't look as valuable. At any rate, I took the entire display of cards home, stamped sentiments in them and promptly sold them all.

Speaking of greeting cards, you *can* make money by selling your handmade cards at craft fairs. Often, I see sellers who have way underpriced their cards because they view the mass-produced cards that can be found in every store on any block in their town as competition. This is a mistake. You're not a mass-market producer; you don't have to try to compete with them.

Sure, a potential buyer may pick up a handmade card and say, "Wow! Six dollars! That's a little too expensive for me," and put the card down. Then she might stop on the way home and throw a boring mass-produced card for $4.99 into her cart and not even notice the price on the back. I don't get it, but you shouldn't focus on this buyer. Instead, focus on the multitude of buyers at the craft fair who expect to pay more for quality handmade items.

A note of caution: If you decide to use rubber stamps to stamp anything on the cards that are for sale, make sure the manufacturer is an "angel company." That means that they allow you to use their images to sell your hand-stamped items. Some rubber-stamp companies don't want you to sell anything with their images or photocopy their images for obvious reasons, so don't do it! You can find the company's policies in its catalogs, on their Web sites, by e-mail or by calling them on the phone.

You may think that it's a crazy policy as a rubber stamp is a tool. But to the artists who drew the images for them, it's copyrighted work, and many of them don't want you to make money off their work. Some feel that a small ease in this direction will lead to further infringements,

Tips for selling at a show

*By Carol Ramsey,
owner of Stampotique*

1. Choose something that you're really good at. Like to work with clay? Painted junk? Pick one craft and go forward with that. Don't muddy it with other sidelines. Keep your focus. Maybe you would like to make scrapbooks for people?

2. Set a conservative sales goal. If you're expecting to make a lot of money right away, you might be disappointed, then get discouraged, and quit. Take it slow, but make a goal. Once that goal is reached, then you can raise your expectations and set another goal. Remember to keep your goals attainable. When you achieve a goal, you feel good about yourself and your craft, and you look forward to moving ahead. Attainable goals keep negativity out of the picture.

3. Don't let others discourage you. Listen to your heart. It's better to have tried than to always wonder what if? Go forward. Make your art and then rent a booth!

4. Don't be discouraged by competition, although do be informed of it; know it and learn from it. It's a great teaching tool. Don't be ruled or frightened by competition. Step forward and always continue to be the very best you can be. If you dwell on what others are doing, you use up quality energy that should be put into your own business. Negativity in any form is hurtful. Think positive thoughts, surround yourself with positive people, and keep your trade upbeat.

5. You need to find a niche for your work, be it selling out of a basket at work or visiting boutique shops in your town. Will the boutiques entertain consignment? What percentage of the retail price will they reimburse you? Are you prepared to give them a figure? Put together a wonderful, exciting, and mouthwatering portfolio! If you plan to sell cards at work, maybe a lovely three-ring presentation binder is what you need, full of page protectors packed with beautifully designed cards and envelopes that customers can choose from. If you have specific samples you won't be expected to waste half your time trying to come up with something new. You simply replicate the design they want. You are saving time, thus making your time more profitable! Remember that the presentation and packaging of your product make a difference, too!

6. Observe and listen to the public. Are they more interested in clip-on earrings or French wires? Do they prefer to buy individual cards or gift packs? What about holiday cards? What will you do if someone asks you to make one hundred Christmas cards? Are you ready for that? What will you charge? Hopefully you're in tune with what the public is willing to pay.

How I learned about "angel companies"

When I found rubber stamping, I wanted to submerge myself in this exciting field. I took a deep breath and plunged into the business. Needless to say, I was still very green and had little experience in any of this big-time sales stuff. For my first official "Sandra McCall" table at a rubber-stamp convention, I wanted to sell my handmade fabric pins. ERA Graphics had some crazy humanoid images that I wanted to use on my dolls. I found the owner's name and e-mailed her to see if it was all right for me to use her images. No answer. Then I wrote her to see if it was OK. No answer. Well, the show was looming, so I used the images and hoped for the best. First mistake. If you're in doubt, don't do it.

So, I get to the show, and whose booth was right next to mine? ERA Graphics! I couldn't believe my eyes! I started shaking from head to toe, knowing that Roberta may very well insist that I take every item that I had made with her rubber stamps off my table. It would have been her right if her policies prohibited others from selling items made with her images.

The first second I spotted Roberta, I went up and talked to her. I explained my dilemma and hoped that she would keep that smile on her face. As it happened, she couldn't have been nicer. She said that her mother had just passed away and that's why I didn't hear from her. She said that she was sorry and that she had not been taking care of business. Well, I could certainly understand that, and Roberta was as gracious as could be, even complimenting my pins. But, boy, that was a huge lesson learned!

such as outright copying of their images for all sorts of reasons. People do steal images, so you can understand the closed policies.

Marketing

Don't worry; you don't have to go to college to learn to be a marketing genius and succeed at making money with your art. Marketing is just a fancy word for checking out what the other guy is doing, what people want to buy and how much they'll pay for it.

At every chance, take a look around you. Walk the aisles at gift shops, craft stores and craft fairs. Peruse magazines and their advertisements. Pore over catalogs. Buy trade magazines such as *The Crafts Report* and read them. What's in right now? What trends do you see that clue you in to what's on the horizon? What are others selling? What are people buying? What are people paying?

It's your job, not to check out the other guy and pilfer his ideas, but rather to look at the other vendors and then figure out what seems to be missing from the market. Then you can focus on supplying what no one else has. When you're looking for answers, keep yourself in mind as the consumer, too. If you're looking for a particular item and can't find it, chances are that hundreds of others are looking for the same thing. So, when deciding what to sell, picture yourself at a fabulous show where all things handcrafted are available. Which aisle will you head down first? What special thing are you looking for?

Salesmanship

Not only are you selling your wares when you sell face to face, but you're also selling yourself. Dress the way that you want to be perceived.

Move around in your booth. Don't just sit in your booth reading or staring off into space. Greet customers with a pleasant smile. You're happy to see them, remember? Rearrange your goods in downtimes. Drinking is fine, but don't eat in your booth. There's nothing worse than food smells if you're not the one eating, especially when the food isn't immediately identifiable.

You may be able to garner more sales by demonstrating your art or craft. I have demoed at several booths, both my own and other vendors'. It's almost always a sure way to move a product. People are more interested in items that are shown to be fun or useful. Also, people are always intrigued by a booth that has a small crowd gathered around it. If you can get your viewers to laugh or applaud, even better. Everyone at the show will look over and want to know what the excitement is about. Be sure to have someone who can handle the register for you if you decide to demo.

Remember to resist the urge to reprice your work during a show, even if it doesn't seem to be moving at the moment.

Shows

You can find listings of shows through trade magazines such as *The Crafts Report*, many hobby and craft magazines, through the various chamber of commerce offices and the Internet. It's so easy to find hundreds of shows these days. The hard part is figuring out which are the good ones. You will find advice on this subject in chapter ten.

One good thing about doing shows is that you can get lots of exposure. You get your name and face out there so people begin to recognize you and your work. You can also observe the buying public in person and gain a valuable marketing advantage. And, of course, every time you vend, you become a little bit more relaxed and a better salesperson.

Preparation

Some show promoters charge a percentage of your sales, some charge a flat space rental, and others charge you a combination of the two. Some shows even charge you a minimal processing fee whether you get approved as a vendor or not. Be sure you understand what you're paying before you go; and understand what you're getting for your money. What's your booth size? Does the space include tables, chairs, table covers, electricity? Is it indoors or outdoors? Do you need protection from the elements? Do you need company signs or does the show provide signs to display over each vendor's space?

If you're strapped for cash, you can actually make a lot of sales space with just a six-foot table. There's nothing wrong with bringing bookcases or cubes that you can stack and that will fit in your space, either on top of the table or on the floor behind you. Make sure you don't exceed your floor space or invade the other vendors' spaces, though.

Get to the show and check in early. What's that? You only have a six-foot table and a few small items and books to sell? Well, I said that once, too. So, I breezed in at the last moment of one show only to find that the promoter had given my table away, thinking I wasn't going to show up at all. It's bad for business to have empty tables at shows, so promoters avoid that if they can. They weren't happy when they had to scramble to find another table for me. I was left in a panic and had to set up when the doors were open and the public was pouring in. To avoid miscommunication, check in with the promoters early.

Here's another reason to get to a show to set up early. I vended a show in Cleveland a few years back. Again, I only rented a six-foot table since I had just a

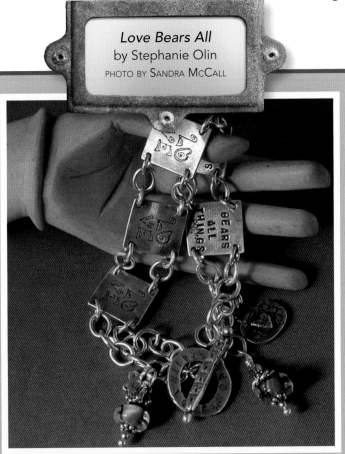

Love Bears All
by Stephanie Olin
PHOTO BY SANDRA McCALL

Be cheerful and interested in the customers, making each one feel special no matter how large or small her purchase is. Have someone help you in your booth so you can take some time to interact. Sales can get hectic, which is great, but that cuts down on customer-interaction time.

– Stephanie Olin,
rubber-stamp and jewelry designer

small amount of jewelry to sell. The promoter knew I was present because I taught classes at the convention earlier. So, I showed up at the last minute to find that my table was still there, but it was completely blocked in on both sides by my vending neighbors. Companies with large setups flanked me and I could see that it would have been a hassle for them to rearrange their spaces. I knew that I would not be able to continually crawl in and out from under the table. So, the promoter found me a four-foot table so that I wouldn't have to crawl under to face the buyers. The promoters weren't happy with me to have to scramble for another table, and I wasn't happy with *anyone* about my space encroachment—it could all have been avoided if I had just shown up early to set up. Learn from me and get there early!

Merchandising and displays

Selling through fairs, shows and conventions requires good merchandising. The best advice I can give about displays is to do a dry run at home. Set up your booth to resemble your rental space as closely as you can. If you have tables, dress them with cloths, props, lighting and your wares. Arrange everything as you would like to see it at the show and then take a photo. When you go to the show, you'll have a picture reference and setup will be a snap.

A simple display is fine; you don't have to go to extremes. But, there are a few important things to consider when designing your showcase. If you have a table, bring a tablecloth if one isn't provided. Make it a plain cloth with no bold patterning and be sure to have it in a color that complements your art. You want your wares to

Rosalita and Octavio
by Olivia Thomas
PHOTO BY LYNDA STONE

Merchandising isn't as daunting as you may think. Spend a little quality time browsing a few trendy boutiques, and note how the displays are accomplished. What made you look? Then try to translate some of these ideas to your needs. Displays are like any composition; the same design elements apply, only on a dimensional scale. Add striking color, a touch of whimsy, and the unexpected.

– Olivia Thomas, *mixed-media artist and folk-art doll maker*

stand out more than your tablecloth. Make it a cloth that will reach all the way to the ground. That way, you can hide cardboard boxes and other paraphernalia under the table.

Bring a small folding table to hold your cashbox or register. Set it on your side of the table next to your chair. This keeps the cash away from the front of your booth, gives you a place to write notes and receipts and gives you more display room. A TV tray is good because it lowers the cash box a little, keeping it further separated from the main display.

If you have small items such as jewelry, you may wish to extend the height of your table to bring it closer to your customers' eye level. A simple way to do this is to make table leg extenders. You can make lightweight extenders by cutting four pieces of PVC pipe to the desired height. Stick them on the existing table legs and you have instant extenders. I learned that trick from Barbara McGuire.

If electricity is available, you may want to consider bringing small clip-on halogen lights. These work beautifully to bring out the sparkle in jewelry or ceramic pieces. The bulbs can get hot though, so place them so that no one gets burned and so the area around your display isn't uncomfortably warm.

Use lifts to make multiple levels for your displays. Lifts can be anything: wood, Lucite, or metal boxes, baskets, or just cardboard boxes placed under the tablecloth. Think creatively about your lifts; look around the house to see what you've got on hand. Remember that lifts mean more to move or ship, so don't make them too heavy. I try to use whatever I packed my goods in as the lifts. Think about displaying your items in bowls, baskets, or trays as well.

Arrange your art on slight angles and face the angles toward the center of your booth. This will draw the buyers' eyes in to your area. Group items together in artful arrangements and leave negative space between them. The customer needs a place to rest her eyes now and then. Work to avoid a booth that looks cluttered and chaotic.

You can use mini knockdown shelves for your tabletop and full-size ones for the sides of your booth if you have the room. Cubes can be used to transport items as well as to stack and build into your display arrangement.

If you're stumped by making arrangements, picture your favorite gift stores—maybe even take a trip downtown. Notice the colors, the props, the displays, and arrangements. Figure out what it is that makes this store attractive to you. Then apply their aesthetic to your wares. Check out stores and books about displays for more ideas on designing your sales area.

Make a tabletop sign with your company's name on it and list the types of payment you accept. If people see a sign that says you accept credit cards, they may make larger purchases.

Credit cards

Accepting credit card payments really does lead to higher sales. The problem is that the large credit companies don't want to waste their time on what they perceive to be small sales. But, take heart; there are many credit card companies that cater to the professional craftsperson, to the sometimes salesperson, and to the weekend crafter. You can find plenty of listings for these companies through word of mouth (ask other crafters), by searching the Internet and from advertisements placed in craft news magazines such as *The Crafts Report*.

I chose to deal with PayPal because of the testimony of a friend who sells on eBay. To have what PayPal calls a "virtual terminal" is quite easy. You sign up for PayPal and the virtual terminal, and they charge you a minimal monthly fee and a very small percentage of all your credit-card sales. The good thing about virtual terminal is that you can take credit card information from anywhere, such as in person at remote craft shows, over the phone or over the Internet. Then you enter the credit card number and purchase information into your computer when you get home. When you enter this information, it's immediately accepted or declined. I may just be lucky, but all of my declines have occurred because I typed the information into the computer incorrectly. PayPal will tell you, in big red letters, exactly where your problem is, so it's very easy. There is, of course, the risk of giving away merchandise to fraudulent people. So, if you have electricity available in your show booth or you have a wireless connection on your laptop, you can run the credit card and ring up the sales while the customer and your art are right in front of you.

Your policies

When you sell, you need to decide what your policies are regarding returns and guarantees. These policies should be stated as often as possible, on your Web site, on your catalogs, sales slips and on invoices. And Stephanie Olin suggests setting a policy sign near the cash register. My return policies are stated as such: All returns must be made within fourteen days. Merchandise must be returned in the condition in which it was received for a full purchase refund.

And my shipping policy is this: In-stock items will ship within one week of order placement. If an item isn't in stock, you'll be notified so that you can decide whether to cancel or place the item on backorder. Custom orders will have a variable shipping time to be determined at the time of purchase.

Some people place the "you break it, you buy it" signs in their booths, but I just think those signs are rude. Breakage is rare, and it's caused by accidents. It's heartbreaking, but I believe that you have to make allowances for accidents—it's the price of doing business.

Essie May
by Olivia Thomas
PHOTO BY LYNDA STONE

CHAPTER 10
Choose Your Venue

Once a tailor, now an artist

Olivia Thomas, mixed-media artist and folk-art
doll maker

*My primitive-folk-art doll business started as a
surprise. I owned a tailor shop and retail store
at the time, and created several folk-art pieces
to have on hand for sale. Some funky, painted,
wooden Halloween pins were a part of this
selection. A rep for a Los Angeles showroom
frequented the store, spied the pins and took
photos. She thought her boss would be interested. He was, and my wholesale business was
born. So I had three businesses to juggle. Due to
issues of shifting interest, demand and econom-
ics, I eventually closed the storefront and pur-
sued the wholesale business on the home front.
Working from home has terrific advantages; no
commute, working in my pajamas and taking
a nap when I need to refresh. The downside is
that I work all the time! But I do what I love,
and I pinch myself that I'm succeeding. I have
slowly expanded my line since the beginning.
The more I offer, the more excitement that's
generated with larger orders to follow. I have
experimented with different creative ideas,
which is a great way to learn your strengths.
I base my designs on what catches my interest
or makes me giggle. I love Halloween, so it is
difficult not to continually create items for this
season. In the end, design and build what makes
you smile, and it will make someone else smile.
Energy is always in motion, and my wholesale
direction shifts continually. Growing the business
is a constant challenge. I am more overwhelmed
each year with the holiday orders. I always ask
myself one question: How can I do this smarter?
A few ideas: encourage orders well in advance
of need, find conscientious help to assist at
busy times, stay organized, focus and replenish
energy by not working occasionally! Balance!
I occasionally do private shows and art-venue
shopping days. I sell my limited-edition and one-
of-a-kind work to galleries and shops. The more
demanding my wholesale business becomes the
harder it is for me to take the time to make art.
I know I need to do it. From this artistic expression springs new ideas for my line.*

There are so many different types of craft shows, stores and other venues for your art. It takes time, trial, and error to find the right outlets for you. I've outlined a few options here. Most gallery and store buyers are very beginner-friendly. They want to satisfy their customers, so they're continually searching for new products and are happy to see new faces on the art scene. They're waiting for you, so just breathe, gather your courage and make appointments. Send preview information about you and your work. Include good, clear photos or slides. Before you waste anyone's time, make sure you can produce what you're hawking. If a buyer asks for two dozen of an item by a certain date, be realistic about your ability to supply that buyer. I've heard over and over that the most frustrating part of a buyer's job is when artists neither ship on time nor provide what they promised. Most buyers will want to work with you, but you may come across some grouchy duds. It's normal—don't let it discourage you.

Fairs and local bazaars

A good place to get your feet wet is to line up a few craft bazaars or fairs. They help you get over the fear of dealing directly with buyers, give you insight into the world of tabletop display and allow you to overhear comments about your work that can be informative in your creative life to come. You'll most likely be stationed right next to another vendor, so you can chat and gather even more information about sales venues.

However, fairs and local bazaars will probably not be your ticket to success.

The problem with these sales venues is that their main focus is different from your agenda. These events are generally about entertainment first. They exist to make money for an organization. For instance, bazaars are established to make money for a church or school. In the case of fairs, people go to socialize and to be entertained and fed, but they don't necessarily go to buy art. Fairs and bazaars can be good for you if you have several inexpensive items that coordinate with the event. Maybe you can make souvenirs or keepsakes that people can buy to commemorate their day.

Craft malls

Craft malls are stores that rent shelf space so that artists can sell their handcrafted wares. There are even craft malls that sell over the Internet these days. The best part about Web-based malls is that you don't have to walk the aisles!

A physical craft mall works like this: You call to set up an appointment with the owner or manager and then go into the store with some of your samples and your port-

Unexpected venues

By Sarah Fishburn, collage artist

Be open to unexpected venues. I've participated in several shows (sales) at my local Whole Foods market. Although it's an everyday community gathering spot for shopping, meeting friends or just grabbing a quick bite, they also have a lovely space in the Cooking School, which isn't always occupied. Our shows are on a Friday night for three hours, and with yummy treats, a little background music and something for every-sized purse, artists and customers all leave satisfied.

Donate your art to causes you support. At auctions and other fundraisers, you can provide detailed contact information and often your cards. The lucky person who takes home your art may just contact you again. Those who weren't quite so lucky have at least seen your work and will also have a means to get in touch with you.

Many medical providers are no longer satisfied hanging the same old art. Some have also begun displaying art not just in waiting areas, but also in exam rooms. Let them know if you have pieces, which could meet their needs!

We all love to give gifts of our art to friends. They can become our most avid art advocates! Let them know you don't mind at all if they go on and on about that fabulous necklace you made, and then pass on your contact info to all admirers.

Secret Be Kind
by Sarah Fishburn
PHOTO BY SARAH FISHBURN

Prices for retailers

*By Carol Ramsey,
owner of Stampotique*

If someone has something to sell, show me. Give me a call, e-mail, whatever. Bring in the product. If it needs to be packaged, have it in the package. Present it to me as you would want it presented to the public. Be forthright with the wholesale price and the recommended retail price. I want to price the item just as other shops are pricing it. Do you wholesale to the big box stores? Do you sell on the Internet and if so, at the same price as I would be selling the item? In other words, I don't want to be undercut by the wholesaler. Why should I try to sell the item at regular retail price while the other person is selling on the Internet or through a buying club for dollars less? I'm open to teachers, too. I may prefer that the teacher sell her items directly in the classroom, though. If that is the case, I expect the teacher to come to class with her own cash to take care of purchases. I'm pretty open on that.

folio. They tell you how much space rental costs, and some take a percentage of your profits as well. Check with them to see what their loss policy is. If something of yours is stolen, misplaced or damaged, will you be reimbursed in any way? It's likely that the mall doesn't claim responsibility for any of these things. Think about it. That may be too risky for your type of craft. You'll probably be required to "walk the aisles" once or twice a month as well. This can actually be beneficial. You can keep an eye on your booth, listen to what customers are saying about the mall and, possibly, learn what they're saying about your own space.

You'll be responsible for decorating your space—most malls let you paint it and merchandise it in any way you like. You'll also be responsible for pricing your items, restocking your space and keeping it up. Go in often to check on your space. I didn't imagine how messy beautifully stocked shelves could look after only one day of sales. People pick things up and carelessly set them down—often not even in the right booth. This happens all day and every day that the store is open for business. The mall is responsible for making the sales, supplying you with an itemized listing of what has sold and then paying you with a check, usually once a month.

The good news is that you don't have to be at your store every day, someone else is doing the bookkeeping for you (to an extent), and you don't have to run the cash register. This gives you more production time. The bad news is that you're not at your store every day, someone else is doing the bookkeeping, and you're not running the register. You have to trust in the people who run the mall. For this reason, you should keep an accurate inventory of what goes in and out. If something is missing, don't jump to conclusions too fast. Many times, customers pick up an item, change their minds about buying it and then set it down wherever they happen to be. Check the other booths—you'll probably find the missing goods on someone else's shelves.

To find craft malls, check magazines such as *The Crafts Report*, check your town's yellow pages and search the Internet. When you find a mall, it isn't rude to ask for referrals. If they're hesitant to let you contact someone who sells their art there, then look elsewhere. Bad management runs rampant through craft malls, both the physical sites and the ones on the Web. That's not to say that there are not far more good malls than bad, but just be aware of the risks.

Approaching galleries

By Sarah Hodsdon, mixed-media collage, note-card and rubber-stamp designer and instructor

I approach galleries much like I approach manufacturers or any other potential client. I think what most artists miss is the fact that they need to offer their clients something of value. Galleries are in business to make money. They have limited wall space and they will choose their exhibitors with a very discerning eye. It is always smart business to do the research and know as much about that establishment before you even step foot in the door. I always send the gallery a press kit or literature about me. I include a letter of introduction that also explains why I want a space on their wall and what benefit I bring to their gallery.

I write down on my calendar the day I send a piece to a gallery, add a few days and then make sure I call them and personally ask about the pieces I sent (this turns a cold call into a warm call). I ask for a time when we can meet so I can show them a portfolio of my work, and I always send a thank-you note. In the event that I don't get into the gallery, I always make sure to send them regular updates when my work is published and keep them abreast of the various exhibits or projects I may be working on as a courtesy. You never know when they will see something and call you out of the blue.

Sunset
by Sarah Hodsdon
PHOTO BY SARAH HODSDON

Retail craft or art shows

There are basically two different types of shows: public and juried. In public shows anyone can apply for a space without first showing their wares for juried approval. Booth and table spaces are filled on a first come-first served basis. As the name suggests, a juried show is one in which you must provide photos of your work and gain approval for acceptance into the show. You need exceptional photos of your work to show the board, because the competition is fierce.

There are pros and cons to each type of show, but the common advantage to doing any show is that you come away with a large amount of cash rather than having to wait for a gallery or store to pay you. You also have person-to-person interaction and can observe the response to your art immediately. Shows are good testing grounds for new merchandise.

However, there are marked differences between public and juried shows. It's easier for the beginning artist or crafter to get into a public show. The price of a booth rental is usually less for a public show than for a juried show because the advertising is not as aggressive and the reputation not as impressive. In a public show with lower admission, there are more people who attend "just to look." The price of admission is generally higher at a juried show, so more serious buyers attend. Also, juried shows have a reputation for selecting only the best exhibitors, so they usually have higher attendance than public shows. The buyers expect to see higher prices at juried shows, therefore they may perceive the wares to be of higher intrinsic value. That may mean more sales for you.

Some of the cons of shows are the high cost of shipping your wares across the country, the hassles of all the schlepping, several exhausting days of glad-handing, time away from your studio, travel expenses and breakage and loss.

Galleries

One of the downsides to selling wholesale or on consignment at galleries and stores is that you don't get your money as soon as the item sells. There can be a thirty- to ninety-day lag time, sometimes longer. You do have the right to state in your sales agreement that you wish to be paid upon receipt of invoice. However, not many people pay attention to that time frame these days.

Stores

Sole proprietors own most small stores. They're the most realistic stores for you to approach if you're making items by hand. A large chain store requires you to make multiples of the same item and often in large quantities that you may not be able to produce. It's also unlikely that they want to buy from you since they prefer to go overseas to buy from people whose cost of living isn't as great as yours.

Museum stores

Almost every museum has a shop that stocks everything from greeting cards to high-end art. It isn't difficult to sell to a museum store, but there are a few things to keep in mind if this is your goal.

Most museums have a definite direction. For instance, some specialize in natural history, some in fine arts and others in living history. There are many, many types of museums, so you must take care to match your art with the right museum. In addition, most museums have constantly changing exhibits. It's especially advantageous if you can supply them with items that are related to their exhibits at the appropriate time.

There is usually just one person running a museum store. This person not only orders new merchandise to sell but also acts as manager and counter clerk and is always busy. (This is also true for many gallery or gift-store owners.) So, schedule appointments. Send preview information along with samples if you can. Clear photos are always appreciated. Include information about your studio and your production techniques, especially new or innovative ones. Also, include a short bio or history of yourself as the artist. If you can, design printed material such as colorful postcards that the museum can display. Include information cards that can be tucked in with customers' purchases. Most museum stores are small and space is in high demand, so museum buyers want to be sure that your product will sell before they buy from you. You don't have final control over how your item is displayed in any shop, but you may be able to influence it by providing your own portable display. If you can add to the display to make it more interesting or even if you can supply cool postcards that the shop can offer to their customers, it's more likely that the museum buyer will see your product as profitable for them. Actually, any printed material that you supply may be included in museum catalogs or advertisements. That means more exposure for you!

Merchandise found in museum stores ranges from ten dollars to thousands of dollars. They want to attract the casual browser as well as the art-collecting enthusiast. The museum store buyer is often looking for new and unique artworks. They want to snag artworks that have not previously been seen, and they're under a lot of pressure to do so. One of the main reasons for this pressure is that the store's customers are going to museums expressly to see things that they have not seen before. Isn't that why you go to museums? So, think about what is being exhibited and brainstorm for new ideas to go along with the exhibits—exciting ideas that will grab a passerby's attention. The store isn't usually the destination for a museum visitor, so you'll need to provide a reason for them to stop, browse and buy.

There is a show called the Museum Retail Conference & Expo where crafters and artists can exhibit their work directly to buyers. The Association of Museum Stores (AMS) sponsors this annual show. For more information, log on to the Web and check out www.museumdistrict.com.

Coffee Talk
by Claudine Hellmuth
PHOTO BY CLAUDINE HELLMUTH

CHAPTER 11
Find Other Outlets

Licensing your art
By Claudine Hellmuth, collage artist and author

Many people ask me during my workshops how I got into licensing my artwork and how they can do it, too. For those of you who don't know what licensing is, it's when an artist sells the rights to a company to reproduce her artwork on a product. In exchange the artist usually receives a royalty, which is a percentage of the money made from the product. Licensing can be a hairy business. With contracts, agreements and percentages, it can be confusing. I'll tell you everything I know about the wild world of licensing and hopefully it will help you avoid some of the pitfalls and enjoy many successes!

During the past seven years I've managed to get my art on twenty-five different kinds of products—on blankets, pillows, drink coasters, magnets, greeting cards and more. How I got started was actually pretty simple. I'd been creating collages and artworks, but I was too attached to them to sell the originals. One day someone said to me, "Your work would be great on cards," and I thought, Yes! That would be wonderful! I could make money and still keep the artwork.

Next I needed to find companies that might want to license my artworks. I began by buying a book called the Artist's and Graphic Designer's Market (F+W Publications). This book lists all the various companies interested in licensing art, from greeting card companies to toy companies. It's an amazing resource that includes company names, what kind of art they are interested in,

the addresses and important people to contact. It has become my bible. I still use it to find companies. A new issue comes out every year, and I recommend getting the current issue so you have all the correct contact information.

Once I got my first copy of this book, I carefully went through each and every listing. If I found one that looked like it might be a good prospect I placed a sticky note next to it. I did this throughout the whole book. Then I looked at the Web sites of the noted companies to make sure my look would fit in with theirs. If I found one that might be a good match and they had e-mail contact information, I sent an e-mail inquiring about their interest and included a link (never attaching images) to my Web site. It was amazing how often I got a response simply from sending an e-mail. It didn't cost me a thing—only my time! If I sent a company an e-mail I wrote on the sticky note when I sent the e-mail, and then I wrote when I heard back. If the company didn't accept e-mail submissions, I created a packet for them. I bought glossy folders from a stationery store and added a few color copies of my artwork and my business card. I also pasted a smaller color copy of my favorite piece to the front. This created a nice presentation that cost about six dollars per packet. After I sent a packet, I marked in the book when I sent it, and if I heard back as well.

This is the easiest way to get started in licensing. All it takes is your time and a small amount of money.

Sweetheart Pearl
by Lisa Pavelka
PHOTO BY LISA PAVELKA

Branching out

By Lisa Pavelka, polymer-clay artist

Becoming an artist was my second career. I left a position as a television producer/director so I could stay home with my small children and continue to make a financial contribution to the family. It began with a figurine line I sculpted from clay. Most of the line consisted of miniature bears: thus the name Bearly There. My plan was to return to television once my youngest child entered school full time. I realized that continuing to work from home would afford me greater flexibility and freedom to remain active in my children's lives.

With more time on my hands, I began to experiment with more complex artistic concepts. It was around this time that I attended my first art industry trade show. I went in the hope of finding better wholesale resources for the materials I used for my figurine line because the Internet was not viable yet. I

approached the company that manufactured the polymer clay I used. After showing them my work, they asked me to work as a freelance designer. With their encouragement, I began submitting project articles for publication. That snowballed into writing books, doing DVDs and appearing on television.

I found I was increasingly frustrated at not finding the type of products I needed, which led to the development of my own product lines. Some are self-financed while others are licensed to other companies.

It's OK to be multidimensional in what you do, but don't start out trying to sell, teach and write all at once. Pick an area to focus on and then give it plenty of time to determine if it's right for you. Once you've honed your skills, you can decide if you wish to add another dimension to your career, try a completely new direction, or stick with what works. Most people function best when they concentrate their skills in one direction. Others thrive on the challenge of balancing multiple pursuits at the same time.

Become a craft designer

A craft designer comes up with new ideas and gets paid by submitting them to magazines for publication or to manufacturers to be included in their advertising campaigns. Craft companies are always on the lookout for top-notch craft designers. They need someone who will enhance the look and the uses of their products, and are willing to pay for it, because it moves their product. If you use their materials to write your books and articles and you use them in your classes, the students want to buy the products, so it's great advertising for the manufacturer. If you have an idea that will increase the sales of a company's product, believe me, they want to hear about it. Most manufacturers also reward the craft designer with free materials in addition to monetary payment.

Develop new products

If you have an idea for a product that's not yet on the market, approach companies with your vision. I did this when I found that I loved rusting everything in sight with a two-part chemical product. I didn't like the fact that it really was rust and would therefore continue to degrade as rust does. I was already using JudiKins products in my books and classes, so I was very familiar with them and their artist-endorsement program. I contacted them and asked if they would be able to concoct an embossing powder that was pitted and would look old and textured—kind of like rusty metal. Judi Watanabe, the owner, was excited about the idea and thus the line of Rustique embossing powders was born, based on my unique mixture of powder and inclusions. I'm being paid for that idea, and you can get paid for your ideas, too!

Prickly Pear Botanical
by Sarah Hodsdon
PHOTO BY SARAH HODSDON

To license or not to license?

By Sarah Hodsdon, mixed-media collage, note-card and rubber-stamp designer and instructor

Licensing your artwork is one of those things that I'm still unsure about. It's a weird beast. Yes, to have your name on something is cool, but it comes with a huge price. When you put your name on a product, you shift from being neutral to someone who has a vested interest and an agenda. I didn't really think about that aspect until it was already done. If I could do it all over again, I definitely would reconsider some things. When your name is on a product, you have to push your product. If the product becomes obsolete or falls out of favor, you're forced to reinvent yourself or fade away as the next style or product comes on the market.

Also, you no longer have your students' best interest in mind. They pay you to teach and to give them the most up-to-date information. They expect you to tell them what to invest their money in, and aid them in choosing the right materials for their journey, not just the things that will line your pockets. Crafting dollars in the budget are precious. I need my students (the ones paying my paycheck) to know that they're not going to receive an infomercial when they come to class—they're going to use the products and materials that are best suited to what we are making. I love the stamps I made and I'm so proud of them, but I'm a rubber-stamp addict and I simply adore too many others to push only my own.

There's nothing wrong with licensing your handiwork, but I think you need to really do some soul searching about what you intend to do, what you want from your career and what the potential outcomes are (good, bad and ugly) before you do it. I'm perfectly content being in the background designing this or that—then I can use my products without feeling I have to push them.

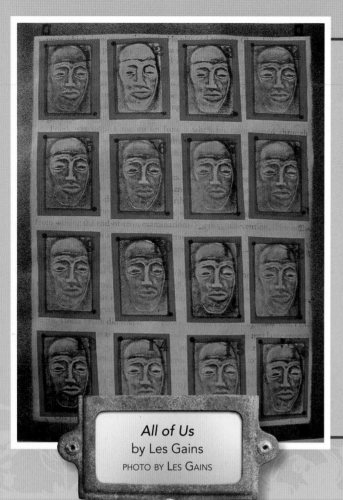

All of Us
by Les Gains
PHOTO BY LES GAINS

We (Arthouse525) held our first weekend of classes in the ghost town of Jerome, Arizona in November 2006. We had a handful of daring artists come from different parts of the country to learn our resin casting methods, screen-printing techniques and collagraphy print making. It was a great time for all of us. The biggest joy for me was to see the look in the students' eyes and the smiles on their faces when they created their experimental works of art. It was at this time that I saw a purpose for the paths I had taken. And it made me smile.

– **Les Gains,** *photographer, collagraphist and sculptor*

To start, look up craft companies and search for their "product development" divisions. Obviously, there are unscrupulous companies that have burned artists by taking their ideas without paying them. So, ask around before you get involved with a company. Get references, if you can. Once you've attended a few trade shows, you'll become familiar with the reputable manufacturers.

Demonstrate at stores and trade shows

The exhibitors at trade shows often need people to demonstrate their products. I have demonstrated product at rubber-stamp stores, craft-trade shows and rubber-stamp conventions. A good demonstrator is a good salesperson, and in demand. My rate is $50 per hour with a two-hour minimum. I believe that's the going rate for this type of position. These jobs are relatively scarce when you consider how many creative people would like to do them. Finding this type of a job is easier after you

start getting a name for yourself. The advantage of lining up a few demo gigs is that it gets you noticed and can lead to television appearances and writing opportunities. For instance, MaryJo McGraw was demonstrating at the JudiKins booth at a rubber-stamp convention when she caught the eye of a North Light Books editor. MaryJo has already written six books with North Light and has contributed to others. Book editors often patrol the craft conventions to see what's new and to scout new authors. To be qualified for this type of work you must have a good working knowledge of the product. Know how far you can push it and think of new, creative and exciting ways to use it. You'll have to answer a lot of questions about the product, so do your homework. You have to enjoy having an audience, too. I'm actually kind of shy, but put me behind the demo table and I would sell my mom if she had a good dress to wear. Just kidding, but you really do have to have that need to impress and make people want what you're showing.

You can find demonstration jobs in several different ways. The organizers of the shows can often match demonstrators with exhibitors. Contact them to see if anyone is needed. Go to the shows with your portfolio, business cards and postcards in hand—you may be able to make connections in that way. Bring samples into craft or rubber-stamp stores and gear your sales pitch to show the owners how they can increase their sales by paying you to demo products for them. It may sound far-fetched, but it works!

Sell patterns and kits

When you come up with wonderful new projects, it may be to your advantage to sell the patterns or kits. Think of all the time you would save if you didn't actually have to labor over finished work. The initial time investment is in the design, of course, but once you have all your instructions written, photos taken and supply lists typed, then it's just a matter of kit assembly. You can charge almost as much for a kit as for the finished project. People pay more for patterns and instructions that they think they can duplicate over and over when they are into making things themselves.

A wonderful place to sell kits and patterns is at craft fairs. Many attendees are there for the sole purpose of cruising the aisles in search of new ideas. They don't want to purchase what you make; they want to copy what you make. So, why not sell them the kit? I often sell both side by side. I price the kit so that it's just a teeny bit less than the finished artwork. I have found that my sales of a finished project are not hampered in any way by having the kit there. In fact, they complement each other and satisfy both types of browsers.

Another good venue is stores. Match the store to your patterns and kits. If you sell patterns for sewing dolls or purses, approach fabric stores to carry your line. If you have developed patterns for creative bookbinding, approach paper sellers or rubber-stamp stores.

Host your own art retreat

As Arthouse525, Les and I hosted an art retreat where we rented several rooms in a small hotel. We were the only instructors. We co-taught four classes over a weekend and had a blast. The fee was structured to include the hotel room and all of the classes and materials. It turned out to be such an energizing art adventure that we are planning on making it a yearly event. Only, next year, everyone will rent their own hotel rooms, and we will only charge them for the classes.

To host your own retreat, you need a place to hold it. Choose a hotel with a large room (or several) for classes, or rent a unique space such as a warehouse. If you're planning a large turnout, check out the convention centers found in most cities. Then you need dates, instructors and a class schedule. The most important item you need is your long mailing list. After you've written your invitation with all of the particulars, you can do a selective mailing or mail it out to as many people as you can. Let them know that the first to pay will be the first ones booked, and that there are only a limited number of spots open.

Sell your drawings to rubber-stamp companies

I sell my drawings to Stamp Oasis and to JudiKins. Stamp Oasis approached me to see if I would sell. I approached JudiKins, and they said yes. It's not that hard—companies are always on the lookout for new, fresh artwork, and if you can draw, you're in demand! It seems that each company pays for drawings differently. Some pay royalties while others pay per drawing.

One thing to make sure of before you agree to sell is whether you still hold the copyright. If you're selling all rights, then set a far higher price for your work because that means you can't ever use the art for anything else. I sell limited rights on my drawings. The company can use my images for rubber stamps, and I agree not to do the same to avoid competition with them. But I can still use the images to print up T-shirts or note cards, for instance.

Start your own rubber-stamp company

If you love drawing, rubber stamping, travelling and talking to people, maybe you should start your own rubber-stamp company. The process is fairly simple. Draw and then scan your images at a high resolution. Clean them up and fine-tune them on the computer if you need to. You can find companies that take your drawings, make a magnesium plate (this is where the high cost is) and then a matrix board so that rubber can be pressed. The rubber sheets are then cut up and mounted onto wood to make a stamp or left whole to sell as an unmounted sheet of images. The magnesium master can run around $90 for an 8" × 10" (20cm × 25cm) sheet. The rubber sheets of the same size are usually only around $8–$10. One custom plate can be quite expensive, but selling multiples of the same image is where you recoup your investment and then start making a profit.

Rubber stamps can be sold to stores wholesale, through mail order, on your Web site and at conventions and shows. If you're a small company, you can make the most money by hitting the road and doing the show circuits. This gets your name out there and people start recognizing you and you soon establish a loyal following of customers. The upside to shows is the interaction with people. There's a lot of energy at the shows, and they're exciting. You have people stationed in booths near you so it's fun to chat and compare notes with the neighboring sellers when there's a lull in the action. And, of course, there are the fistfuls of cash at the end of a show. The downside is that it's exhausting.

The Streetmarket Handmade Book
by Traci Bautista
PHOTO BY MICHAEL VINCENT

CHAPTER 12
Take Care of Business

Persistence pays

Traci Bautista, handmade-book and mixed-media collage artist

My art journey began because I was tired of working in Silicon Valley. Deciding to leave the stability of a well-paying corporate job to become a full-time artist was a huge risk. But I knew there was more to life and work, than marketing software to Fortune 500 companies. After eight years of commuting, traveling the country and wearing business suits, I wasn't passionate about my work and was burnt out, so I decided to make a lifestyle change. I quit my job without a plan. I took time off to travel and figure out what I wanted to do. During my break, I discovered a program to teach elementary art history. I'd always wanted to teach kids art, so I interviewed and landed my first teaching gig. As a traveling art teacher, I taught thirteen classes at various schools, art centers and summer art camps. That was almost five years ago.

During that time I concentrated on making art, something I'd put off for too many years. Also, I discovered there were adult mixed-media workshops. So, I showed my artwork to owners of local stores and my classes were put on the schedule. I then developed new classes,

submitted my work to magazines and applied to teach at national mixed-media conventions. Persistence paid off.

The key to being successful in any career is to live the life you love, being truly passionate about your job. A mixture of hard work, persistence, luck, business knowledge and networking has gotten me to where I am today; with these key elements comes success. Now I live what most would call an unconventional life as an artist painting paper, stitching fabric and doodling for a living. My days are filled with up to twenty hours of work, seven days a week, making art; traveling weekends to teach workshops; having a mobile office from an airplane, Whole Foods Market or Starbucks, e-mailing from my phone; and updating my Web site, blog, MySpace and Yahoo! pages. Balancing life and work is very important to me, so I make time for leisure, hanging out with friends and family, coloring my hair atomic pink and emerald green, taking the occasional break for the gym, yoga, naps in the afternoon and walking the dogs. My job doesn't feel like work. I can say that being unconventional in life and art makes me happy, and it's always an adventure. I wouldn't have it any other way—I love being a free spirit. Do what you love, and the money will follow. Be happy. Live an artful life.

> *I am not organized. I am a messy artist. My studio is in major disarray even though I crave order and am making strides in that direction. From a business perspective, I've learned the hard way; you'll sink if you're not organized.*
>
> *My advice is to employ a trustworthy and business-minded soul who can do this for you. In my case, I am blessed to have my hubby take on this role...and he is so much better at it than I am.*
>
> — **Stephanie Olin,** *rubber-stamp and jewelry designer*

Peace and Love
by Stephanie Olin
PHOTO BY SANDRA McCALL

The dilemma of start-up costs

If you can, keep your day job until you have some money saved. This is a no-frills, but semi-ideal way to start your crafts business. You need funds to pay for at least four months of household bills, including rent/mortgage, car payments, utilities, credit card payments, anything that you have to pay on a monthly basis. Whether you're a sole proprietor or in a partnership, everything that you own is at risk. If your company has financial difficulty then your house, car and any other valuables may be used to settle debts. Moreover, a bad credit rating due to late payments on your personal bills will affect your ability to get business loans. It is all one and the same with your business.

You also need to figure out your start-up costs. These change depending on your business. In my case, I needed enough supplies to teach classes of twelve people so I stocked up on rubber stamps, paper, ink pads and countless other art supplies well before I actually started teaching classes. And, of course, I started stocking the materials well before I quit my accounting job. In your case, it may be that you want to sell jewelry or paintings. No matter what you do, you need supplies and backstock. To do it the bootstrap way, start gathering at least these minimums while you still have a "regular" job.

If you don't have a regular job, don't have any credit, and you need cash now, how do you get it? The same old Catch-22 applies today as it did yesterday: If you have no money, it's hard to get a loan. If you already have money and supplies, companies will start throwing free things at you. It makes no sense, but it's a fact. So, how do you start?

Often, books suggest that you borrow funds from friends and family. Yes, you may be able to ask a family member or a very trusted friend to float you a loan. But I have a few recommendations for you. When you ask for money, make it a specific amount and tell them that you'll pay it back with a "lender's" fee. To be polite, they will most likely tell you that you don't have to, but do it anyway. Specify the time when you'll pay them back and make it a binding contract. Friends and family aren't to be taken advantage of...ever! Even for this transaction, draw up a contract.

I have had verbal agreements with friends and I did pay them back as planned, but I always felt that they were thinking, *Oh no, here she comes again.* The sad fact is that once you borrow, even if it is only one time, you'll feel like a "borrower" and it may not sit well with you. It doesn't with me. So, my advice is to make it legitimate with a contract and pay them back with interest so that they become a "lender," but in a more comfortable and profitable way for both of you. If there ever comes a time when they think your borrowing is a one-way street, they can look at their contracts to see how much money they have made and will have proof that you did pay them back on time. That should even out the field a little. Still, and I know this sounds old-fashioned, if you can avoid borrowing, do it! You'll be happier many years down the road.

Of course, you can throw all this advice out the window if you're lucky enough to have back-up funding from a well-to-do spouse, an inheritance, or you're just independently wealthy.

The wonder of computers

A computer and color printer are musts if you're to make any money. Not only do the various programs make it easier to keep up with paperwork, but you can also make your own hangtags, business cards, printed instructions, etc. I can't imagine trying to make my class handouts with just a typewriter. I would go broke buying buckets of Wite-Out if I had to type everything manually on a typewriter.

If you don't have a computer, take your first earnings (if you can) and buy one. It doesn't have to be expensive, but make sure it's able to run a good art program such as Adobe Photoshop or CorelDRAW. Microsoft Word is my favorite program for writing and FrontPage is what I use to design my Web site. You can buy a computer "bundled" with popular programs. Even if the bundled computer is $300 more than the one with no programs, go for the bundle if it includes the above programs, because each program can run $400 and up.

Most computers will come with standard writing programs and a starter art program. Some even include a small scrapbook program, which are excellent for making cool labels and hangtags, too! Even though you may have to start with lower-end programs, that doesn't mean they aren't powerful. You can do a lot with a simple art or office program.

In addition to a computer, monitor, mouse and color printer, you'll want to be able to send out notices via e-mail. So, you'll need a modem and Internet access. A flatbed scanner and a digital camera with a reader for your computer are other helpful tools.

You can get the old clunky monitors for a song now, so if you can't afford an extra large screen, I recommend two monitors for your computer. Set them side by side, both hooked to the same computer. Together they create one large, inexpensive monitor. You can open Adobe Photoshop on one screen, for instance, and have a word-processing program opened on the other. Then you can just highlight, click and drag your text onto the page lay-

out that you're making in Photoshop or FrontPage. Or, as in the case with Photoshop, there is a "work area" and a lot of little toolboxes. You can drag all the little toolboxes over to the other monitor and have only your working picture area enlarged on one screen with no toolboxes crowding it out. The two-monitor setup is a real time-saver in your design work.

If you have a lot of Web surfing to do, it's faster to have two Internet pages open at the same time. If you have separate monitors, you can see both sites side by side. It isn't only faster to surf, but it also makes comparing information on multiple sites easier.

Nope, this isn't just silly computer stuff from a nerd—it's about working faster and smarter, and that's good for your business.

Ask around, one of your friends may have a used computer for sale that already has all kinds of excellent programs on it. Or they may know someone who does. Most libraries and coffee shops have computers that you can use. Most libraries also allow you to print your materials for a nominal fee. They should also have word-processing programs and even Internet access. Be sure to bring a memory stick or a disk with you so you can save your work.

A good source for programs is eBay. Sealed, unused programs can be found on eBay, but they are a little more expensive than used copies. Still, a brand new program on eBay will run about one-third the full retail price. All of the programs mentioned above are user friendly. I'm not a computer whiz, so if I can do this, you can, too. All it takes, like anything else, is sitting your butt down in front of the computer and doing it!

With your computer you can keep records of inventory, mailing lists, materials used in each item that you sell along with the production costs. You can type letters, item information, class instructions and contacts. You can also design your stationery, hangtags, gift enclosures, sales information, catalogs, flyers, shipping labels and all your forms such as contracts and consignment forms. The list goes on and on, and I can't imagine trying to do it all without a computer.

The agony of paperwork

Paperwork is part of your new deal. In order to make money with handcrafts, you need to keep several records—records for tax purposes, inventory records, resource records, records of what classes you're teaching. Yep, face it; paperwork is an integral part of your new venture. The number one thing to remember about paperwork is to keep up with it. Throwing incoming papers onto a small stack of other paperwork will soon turn into a neglected mountain ready to avalanche. This is part of your work and is just as important to keep up with as any other aspect of earning with creations.

Likewise, writing little cryptic messages on sticky notes and backs of business cards is a bad idea if you make a habit of scribbling and forgetting. Write those notes out in long hand, on your computer or some other designated place, so you won't forget what those marks mean two weeks after you wrote them. Learn from me. I know this, and I still lapse into laziness! It isn't a pretty picture when you pick up a note that just floated down from who knows where and you vaguely remember that this name is important and that you said you would do something for them, but what was it? Who is this, and when did I write this note?

As for paperwork concerning taxes and inventories, if you get befuddled at the very thought of it, or you simply don't have time to do it, you may want to hire help. An accountant or a bookkeeper may be what you need. A part-time secretary may be what you need. Think about how you like to work and then delegate to others what you need to. The right outside help can free up much of your day so that you have more production or design time. I can do my paperwork and all the rest, but I need help with the house, so I have a part-time housekeeper. Just six hours of help, twice a month is all I need to have control of my creative career. Think about what you need and whom you may be able to hire, even if it is a friend or your mom. A little help goes a long way and it just may save your sanity.

The question of price

Pricing an item sounds like it must be the simplest thing in the world. You just take your materials cost, add your labor, then double that and you have a price. Well actually, there is a little more to consider than the cost of materials and your valuable time. So, let's think about production income first. What price should you set on your time? If you pay yourself minimum wage as set by the federal government, your handcrafted items will probably be the most expensive items ever produced. Handcrafts take a lot of time—a lot more time than many potential buyers (and maybe even you) realize. Then, you also have the competition of handcrafted items that are produced overseas where the cost of living may be a lot less than where you're living. So what do you do?

It depends on what the item is. If it is an item that is fun and stimulating enough for me to stay awake making it for two days at a time, then I call that a labor of love and get what I can out of the piece. I sell it for as much as I can, even though I make only 23¢ an hour. But, you can't pay all your bills with "labors of love." So, I cushion the impact with a lot of items that are fast, fun and easy for me to make and that I know I can get far more dollars for than the amount of time and cost that I put into them. You'll probably have to do this, too. Don't feel guilty or think of it as gouging your customers. To survive in the craft world, you need to think of your overall achievements and the bottom line on your profits and losses. Just because the item was quick and easy for you doesn't mean that it has little value, so don't feel guilty about it.

Speaking of guilt, there are browsers who try to negotiate price and try to make you feel stupid or guilty for what you charge. What they don't realize is that you put in a lot of design time, which is the most valuable part. Realize that design is an important aspect of handcrafts. The customer must value that if they want to own one of your items. Don't be ashamed to put a price on your creativity. Don't reduce prices during a show or apologize for your prices. I cringe to think of the times that, in the beginning, I did.

Negotiating prices or changing them during a show leads to confusion and possible loss of customers. Buyers will realize that they should wait until the very end of the show to purchase. They will have seen that you get nervous when it looks like the show is ending and you have not sold as much as you would have liked. Also, people who paid the higher prices will feel cheated, and rightly so. If you have a lot of merchandise left, wrap it up and take it home for another show. You never know what will sell at a particular show. You may sell everything on the first day or you may have to repack and take most of it home. It will sell at another show—that's just the way of it. Don't ever undercut yourself due to a fear that you'll never sell your goods. You'll sell them!

You're also dealing with perception and consumer psychology. Underpricing can be a pitfall. It can lead to a quick sale to some, but it may result in the loss of interest to others. People tend to place more value on what they think is slightly out of their reach. They are also suspicious of the quality of items that they deem too inexpensive. When I was in college, a professor related a well-known story about Pond's to my marketing class.

In 1916, Pond's Cold Cream and Vanishing Cream had been heavy hitters in the cosmetics industry for some time when sales suddenly started dropping and continued to drop. When J. Walter Thompson Company (who was in charge of Pond's advertising) conducted extensive marketing research around 1924, they concluded that the creams "had begun to suffer from their very leadership. Reasonable in price, used by everyone, many women had begun to think that they could not be as good as creams that were more costly or that were imported." (JWT Account History, January 18, 1926)

The campaign blitz that followed was based on elevating the product value by raising the price and hiring celebrities and royalty to give their testimonials about the wonders of the products. The advertising agency established a place for themselves in marketing history when they reached the conclusion that pricing and testimonials from celebrities are directly related to perceived quality. This is an old story but a good one to keep in mind when pricing your work.

Take notice of what browsers are saying. If several have mentioned that your work is fabulous but your prices are awfully low and then put the crafts back on the table, watch and listen to them. As happens many times, an item may not sell if the price is too low. You may have to double or triple your price for the next show.

I applied this pricing principle to my class fees. When I began teaching, I looked around and priced my classes at the same low rate every other teacher was charging. As time went on, I felt that because my class packets contained a lot more information, materials, written instructions and color copies of the project, my classes had a higher value than most of the others. However, by pricing my services at the same level as others, I didn't feel my students fully understood they were getting more from my classes so I nervously raised the prices.

Guess what? More people than ever began to sign up for my classes. Now students and store owners continue to tell me that my classes are still under priced even though I'm at the top of the price structure for teachers. I've found that the higher the price, the more interested the students are and the happier they are to learn something of high value. Why don't I raise the prices even more? Because I know that I'm at the right price when people walk away feeling happy that the class was a good value for their money and I feel that I'm getting paid properly for my hard work as well.

I'm not telling you to gouge your customers. Just don't be afraid to charge what your art is worth, or you run the risk of customers thinking that something is wrong with your class and art offerings.

Unfortunately, there are people who compare your crafts to mass-produced items and say you're overpriced because they can go get a glass platter at such-and-such discount store for a lot less money. Ignore them. They don't get it and never will. These people usually speak out in front of a crowd. When that happens to me, I take advantage of the fact that there are others around. I say (always with a big smile on my face and a wave of my arms), "Move along and stop scaring the customers." Seriously. It always gets a laugh from the crowd and the offending person does move along. Use this opportunity as an excellent time for a soft sales pitch where you point out the time involved in your process as opposed to mass-produced items—it works every time.

The cost of overhead

Of course, you need to consider the cost of materials when you price an item. That's an easy one. The tricky part of pricing is that artists often forget to add in their overhead. You have no storefront so you think you have no overhead. Think again. Overhead is the rent you pay, your utilities, licenses, costs of shipping, travel costs, selling costs like booth fees and any other number of incidentals. Believe it. You do have overhead and, most likely, lots of it.

An easy way to figure your overhead is to take your yearly expenses and divide them by twelve so that you come to a per-month figure. Then divide that by thirty to come to a rough daily amount of your overhead costs. Figure out how much time an item takes you to make in one workday. I don't mean a normal eight-hour workday, but how long you can sit and craft that item in one day. Six hours to make four pieces and then you're cooked? Then, divide your per-day overhead costs by six and that is the overhead per item. That has to be figured in to your selling price. So, a simple formula for pricing is: material cost + overhead + your time = sell price.

My last word on pricing is about a phrase that Donna Kazee in Florida passed on to me: "Don't sell out of your own pocket." It means that just because you can't afford to buy what you make doesn't mean it isn't worth what you're charging. It doesn't mean that other collectors can't afford what you make. The point is that you're trying to make money so that someday you can collect fine items like those that you make, so don't undersell yourself.

The very first collage I sold was to a woman who went nuts over what I had made. She wrote me a check and promptly told me that I charged too little for what I made. She ended up buying many of my pieces and sold them at her gallery for triple the price I charged her.

– **Sarah Hodsdon,** *mixed-media collage, note-card and rubber-stamp designer and instructor*

Acrylic Study
by Sarah Hodsdon
PHOTO BY SARAH HODSDON

Neptune's Daughter
by Roberta Altschuler
PHOTO BY ROBERTA ALTSCHULER

Don't underestimate your value

By Roberta Altschuler, beader, stamp designer and founder of rubber-stamp company ERA Graphics

Some time ago, I was looking for a way to leverage my art. I wanted to do something once and sell it over and over again. I decided to make rubber stamps from the images in my journals, in which I always sketched. In a short time, I had a lovely little stamp business that wasn't piecework. In time this led to cards, which led to collages, which led to collages on fabric with beaded embellishment and then just little beaded amulet bags. And I was back to piecework again.

I was having a ball turning these little bags out, some with faces, hands and feet, which became known as my Bag Ladies. Soon it became obvious that I had way too much inventory laying around and needed to find a way to pay for this glorious addiction, so I decided to try and sell the bags (to buy more beads, of course).

I was traveling the country doing stamp shows for ERA Graphics, and in the late 1990s, I took a few bags with me and put them out on my table amongst the rubber. I had no idea how to price the bags. Like most new artists (I was an old hand at art but was new to beading), I undervalued my work.

I learned a good lesson that day as the other vendors scooped up my bags before the show even opened. At the next show, I really upped my prices and still sold out within the first hour. And I kept raising my prices until I reached that magic place where I felt that my labor and talent were being compensated. Well, sort of. I'm convinced that beaders will never make more than five cents per hour, but there is that point where the traffic will not bear another price jump.

As time progressed, my skills improved and I began to use higher quality materials (read: much more expensive beads and gem stones), I began reaching for different markets and customers—that is, jewelry buyers as opposed to rubber stampers who might only buy an occasional piece of beaded jewelry. My prices increased accordingly. Due to numerous requests, I added beading to my teaching repertoire and have managed to incorporate beading into all manner of projects.

The decision of wholesale and retail prices

Craft shows draw an assortment of browsers. Some of them may be sales reps or owners of stores who are on the lookout for new gift ideas. Be prepared with answers and price lists in case you're asked if you wholesale your work.

Your first inclination may be to back off of wholesaling because you know you'll only get half the price that you sell to the public. Take a minute though. Consider all the time and money that it takes to travel to market on your own. The reality is that wholesaling may save you time and money in the long run. It may free you up to increase your design and production time. Moreover, if you decide to get a sales rep to sell your wares to stores, you'll probably get more sales than you could on your own. You have to pay the rep for her time, of course, but she may have access to accounts that you don't. Weigh the pros and cons, apply them to your situation, then decide whether to wholesale or not.

If you do decide to wholesale your art or sell to other dealers, it is best to price your work from the outset so that you can offer it to wholesale buyers at 50 percent off your suggested retail price. You may think it doesn't make a difference if you sell your merchandise at the same price as you sell to a dealer. What happens when a customer goes in and tells the dealer that she loves the item in his store, but she knows you sell it for half his price? She tells the owner that she will wait and buy it directly from you. Yep, the owner, one of your valued customers, will be mad!

The only time that you may be able to get away with this is to sell in a totally different part of the country, and even that is iffy. You don't want to undercut your stores—they are your customers just as much as the individual at the craft show. And if you have two different pricing structures, what happens if your product gets national attention? Of course you can offer wholesale customers a 30 percent discount; some accept that. But, most have to double the purchase price of an item to cover their overhead and make money.

The benefit of buying wholesale

You can't buy all of your supplies at a retail price and still expect to make money on everything you make. If you just need a few items, then you'll probably have to buy them retail because wholesale sources usually require a minimum purchase amount.

I'd heard that the Craft & Hobby Association was supposed to be the greatest show of new craft materials on earth. Supposedly, you could hook up with all kinds of vendors, hand out your business card and collect their catalogs at the show—one stop shopping for absolutely everything. When I was asked to demonstrate stamping techniques at CHA, I jumped at the chance. I was anxious to be able to take a look at this marvel.

I did learn a lot, but CHA is for buyers of storefronts and other manufacturers. Most vendors there are trying to attract the larger orders, those from stores and especially the huge national chains. CHA is not really for the smaller professional crafter. High entry fees to the show will cut most of us out. In addition, to be a buyer, you have to show a photo of a storefront to become a member. Most of the vendors have higher minimum orders than what most professional crafters will be able to pay. I wouldn't look to these large trade shows for very much except to see what's new.

Knowing what I know now, I recommend that you cruise the Internet, check out magazine ads and ask around for sources. Many people are happy to tell you about all their favorite sources. Some will not, however, so use caution when asking fellow crafters about their sources. Always ask when you're on equal footing, such as at trade shows or classes where you're both attendees. Never ask them or store owners for sources when they're in the process of selling. That doesn't go over well because they're trying to sell to all who enter their arena and that includes you. At that moment, they're not focused on furthering your knowledge so you can buy the same materials to make and sell the same or similar items.

Be professional when requesting catalogs from companies, especially if you wish to conduct wholesale business. For catalog requests, you can often call a company over the phone or contact them through their Web sites. Many companies will send catalogs out to you for free. Some companies charge for their catalogs because they want to be sure that you are a serious buyer. Many who charge for their catalog, but include a certificate that you can put toward your first purchase.

To request catalogs and wholesale information by mail, type up a letter stating exactly what you need and include your business card and your resale number. If you have a professional-looking postcard showing your art, include that as well. If the catalog price has been stated in the company's advertisement, include payment for that also.

The abundance of resources

Local shops often have unique items for sale—items other than the same old imports that you see everywhere else. Smaller shops are more likely to support local artisans as well.

It's in our best interest to keep local, privately owned shops open. I'm still mourning the loss of all the cool fabric stores that used to be in my neighborhood. If you don't support your smaller, independently owned stores, you'll soon bemoan the fact that there's no longer any variety or any stores to which you can sell your own handcrafts or teach your craft classes!

Also, when you support local shops, they pay taxes back into your community. Large chains may not be incorporated into your state, so they pay no taxes that would benefit your community.

Purchase recycled supplies. You can often check the telephone book or the Internet for sources and a city near you to find listings of stores that sell recycled supplies. An excellent example is "Art From Scrap" in Santa Barbara, CA. Businesses donate either used or surplus goods to the store, they're dirt-cheap to buy. They

The wholesale question

By Gloria Page, mixed-media stamp artist

In 1993, I made eighteen bookmarks with three Southwest rubber stamps. These were the simplest things you ever saw. I'm almost embarrassed to think about them! If you can believe it, I had never even seen a rubber-stamp magazine. My mom loves me and anything I make, so she carried those eighteen bookmarks in a brown paper bag, showed them to her boss at the La Fonda Newsstand in Santa Fe, got an order, and we were in business!

We had a huge learning curve, like "What's a purchase order?" and "What's wholesale?" "How much should we charge for these anyway?" We're pretty quick learners and understood that we'd entered into the world of wholesale. We decided that the bookmarks would be $1 each wholesale and $1.95 retail. Orders were placed from different shops in Santa Fe, and life was definitely altered from that point on.

I started with wholesale, so I didn't have the experience of many artists who have a huge crisis over it! I just thought it was cool to be in an art business. Then I thought it was even cooler when I was encouraged to make cards and realized the potential was there to make more products at higher prices. There are many things to consider before doing a wholesale business:

1) Is it worth it? If you sold directly in an art show, you could make full retail. For me, it was worth it because I wanted to make a supplemental income, work at home and have a sense of steadiness in getting and producing orders. There's more predictability in wholesale once you get your accounts lined up and on some kind of ordering schedule.

If you sell in shows, yes, you do make full retail. It's fun and feels rewarding. I did both for years: wholesale orders on a daily basis and juried art shows locally. [Those 10' × 10' (3m × 3m) tents are a whole other way of life for sure, especially when you get rained out!] Doing commission work also brings full retail, and those kinds of endeavors help increase your overall profit margin.

2) If you have a wholesale business, do you need a rep to take care of getting orders while you focus on production? If you're concerned about not getting enough money for your products at wholesale to begin with, and then add paying a rep on top of that…sheesh…will you make any money? It's always a balancing act, isn't it? For years, I worked with a card rep and paid her 20 percent of the wholesale for every order she took. I got tired of paying that, and at one point my husband looked at me and simply said, "Eighty percent of something is better than 100 percent of nothing."

That made the most sense the day I got my single biggest order for several hundred bookmarks and more than eighty dozen cards for the Indian Cultural Center in Albuquerque. I was stunned! A $1600+ order was a big order at that stage in the business. I wrote my rep a nice check. That particular place only worked with reps—I wouldn't have landed that account on my own.

You can have reps and at the same time you can generate your own business—when you get your own accounts they are called "house accounts." Make sure you discuss this clearly with your rep(s) to avoid communication issues over "territories" and things like that.

Whether you like getting out and selling yourself and your artwork, or you hate rejection and would rather have someone else get told "no," or you like being in your studio focused on creative production, make your decision based on who you are and your needs.

3) If you take on wholesale, what do you do if you get too much business and can't fulfill the orders? Even though many artists would consider it a happy problem to be that popular, it's an issue for which you have to be prepared. You don't want to start something that you can't finish. Your reputation is at stake, and that's foundational.

Over the years, I learned to tell my reps what I could produce on a monthly basis, and they learned to handle my orders accordingly. When a big opportunity came up, they contacted me and we discussed how to make it work. I never hired anyone to work for me.

4) Is it boring to make the same thing over and over and over again? This is a personal question and you need to be honest with yourself. Know thyself! If you hate repetition, then forget wholesale, unless you can change your personality because you need or want this so much that you can go beyond yourself.

I still have several wholesale accounts even though my focus for years has been in publishing and other art arenas. I downsized from sixty card accounts with a rep, to twenty without a rep, and now down to three card accounts including the Smithsonian. I have my hands in the handmade card business because I want to keep connected and the Smithsonian account is an honor to still have after all these years. I do one art show with my cards every year in Santa Fe during the summer at Saint John's College and I make full retail there (alumni deal!).

> *I also love to work with recycled "things" that challenge my creativity and going to hardware stores is great fun. Tools and toys of the artist's trade are all around us, not necessarily expensive, oftentimes free and always a joy to "re-arrange." A piece of paper becomes that fabulous "perfect card for that special occasion." A designer shop's discarded remnant of silk becomes a lovely Japanese origami box. A wet chunk of clay...a glistening Raku mirror...the potential is limitless.*
>
> – Gloria Page, *mixed-media stamp artist*

also donate the leftovers from manufacturing. Maybe a company produces neoprene visors and they have a lot of waste after they punch out the visor shapes from the neoprene. Well, all of that leftover material can be really cool for some art projects.

Peruse flea markets and yard sales. Wear comfortable shoes and sunglasses and take water with you. Scour thrift stores and second-hand shops for bits of old fabric, buttons, lace and fibers. Check out military surplus stores for old metal boxes and other cool stuff. Most of these types of stores have a large section of camping supplies. That means cool little plastic bottles and containers.

Check eBay for new and used supplies. When buying through eBay (or any mail ordering for that matter), be aware of the shipping costs that you may have to include in your purchase price. I was elated to win two old typewriters through an eBay auction for only $6 each. I figured that I would cut the keys off of them and scavenge any other interesting parts to be had. Well, those things weigh a ton! I ended up paying $25 each on shipping. A lesson learned.

The beauty of artist-endorsement programs

Some art supply, paper and rubber-stamp companies have what is called an artist-endorsement program. It means that if you use their product in your classes or books, they will supply product to you for free. Times are getting tougher though, so many programs have been cut, however there are still a few companies that practice this method of advertising. They want you to use the product and endorse it—showing and telling people that you do indeed use and like the product. This merchandise isn't really all that free. Your part of the "free" merchandise is that you are indirectly a sales rep for the companies. If you feel shy about asking for product, remember that you're important in passing the word on about it. An excellent teacher can move product faster than most sales reps because she is demonstrating and letting her students

use it. The key is in letting them see how fun or great the product is. Many times, to participate in this type of program, you must have already made a name for yourself. You need to be what they consider a high-profile artist for companies to accept you into their programs.

Some companies will pay you in cash or with product, after you are successfully published and when you send them a tear sheet with their product listed and/or pictured in your article. To find out about the programs, ask to be directed to the correct person in charge of it. They usually fall under the company listing of Sales and Advertising. When you call or e-mail to make contact ask if they have an artist-endorsement program and if they do, ask them to send you the guidelines for their program. Many will send this type of information through e-mail.

Keep in mind that most companies get requests for "free" product every day. Some are short sighted and don't see the advertising value, so they may be a little less than enthusiastic in their response to you, or they're already carrying too many artists. Don't let a negative response take the wind from your sales. Thank them for their time and move on.

When you write your books, not only is their product featured, but they are also listed in the resource section, which may drive more people to their sites. From a working artist's perspective, I can tell you that I wouldn't be able to provide as many and varied materials to my students and I would not be able to produce as many step-outs for my books without this exchange. Therefore, to the companies who provide me with material, I'm loyal and try to do the best sales job that I possibly can.

My last bit of advice on this is to ask only for what you need to do your classes and write your books. Don't be greedy. Remember, this is not really a matter of free goods—you have to do your part in the sales effort for companies to want to continue with this practice.

Ceramic Season
by Sandra McCall
PHOTO BY SANDRA McCALL

CHAPTER 13
Mind Your Paperwork

There are several different lists and records that you need to keep. Here are the ones I use that you might find helpful: e-mail, contacts, mailing, items out, inventory, profit-and-loss statement, product, invoice, purchase orders and sign-up sheets. You'll keep most of these lists on your computer. The e-mail, contacts, and mailing lists are self-explanatory—you just need people's contact information. The other forms and lists can get a little more involved. Most of my records are kept on my computer, but when I first started selling my crafts I used manual forms. I used the "table" function in Microsoft Word to make up my forms, then printed them and kept them in folders or files in the file cabinet. All of these forms are simple and designed by me, and you have my permission to photocopy them or use them to guide you in the design of your own forms on your computer.

You can purchase forms from office supply stores as well, but why not take the opportunity to make up your own and have your company name and logo displayed on them?

Items out list

If you teach classes, you send out sample boards. If you sell on consignment to a shop or you have goods consigned to a gallery, you need a way to keep track of your work. When you send materials or slides to be examined for a juried show, you don't want to lose them. If you send artwork to a magazine for publication, you want a record of it. Do you send promotional samples to stores, catalogs to buyers and advertisements to magazines?

These are the times when you have goods out in someone else's hands, and you want to keep track of them. You need to know the date mailed, what you sent to whom and where. Everything you send out that has to do with your craft should be kept on an "items out" list. You may think you will remember who you sent what to, but, truly, it can get out of hand very fast as your business builds up. Be diligent about filling these lists and forms out. (See page 103.)

Purchase orders

Some companies won't wholesale to you if you do not have a purchase order with a number on it. It is how they keep their records. If you want to buy from them, then you have to comply. Having a purchase order is another way to demonstrate your professionalism. I've produced an example of a simple purchase order form. (See page 104.) Make two copies: one for your records and one for the vendor's.

Invoices

If you sell through the mail or to stores, or you wish to bill for services such as mural painting or teaching, create an invoice. An invoice looks pretty much like a purchase order except it has your terms and shipping information included. Make two copies of invoices, one for you and one for the person you are billing. (See page 105.)

Inventory lists

This is probably my most hated of all the paperwork. It is so simple, but such a #@*! However much you may hate it too, it is imperative for you to keep these records. If you don't, how will you know how many goods you make, sell and lose? Your inventory and the cost of making it are integral to the bottom line of your business health. As usual, a computer program will help you out on this, but it all starts with physical counting. As you bring in goods and as you send out goods, mark it down! That is the only way to stay on top of inventory. Be sure to keep inventory of goods taken to shows, sold at craft malls and sent out for consignment selling. That is how you find evidence of theft, too. You can deduct theft on your taxes, so make a record of it! (See page 106.)

Monthly income and expenditures

This is a biggie—this is your ledger so you have all the necessary figures to transfer to your tax forms including the 1040–Schedule C. This is how you can see, at a quick glance, what your monthly and year-to-date profits and losses are. If you need to supply a banker with a profit-and-loss statement, this is where you get the information. The account numbers are standardized bookkeeping numbers. You can add other accounts to the bottom of the list. Fill in only the accounts that are applicable to you and your business. Keep the receipts of your expenditures and copies of incoming checks and monies to back up your reporting. If you need help in determining which expenditures are applicable to you or you do not understand the headings, consult a bookkeeper, the Internet, your tax booklets or the IRS. (See page 107.)

Profit-and-loss statements

I know, you are probably thinking that you are not going to need such a high-minded sounding form for your small venture into the world of selling handcrafts. That's exactly what I thought. I am not a big corporation or even a medium-sized company. Why on earth do I need this?

Well, shock of shocks—it happened that I did need a profit-and-loss statement to prove to a bank that I was making money when I had no W-4 forms to show for it. When I was asked to provide this statement, I panicked. I imagined the multi-paged, glossy statements that I had seen from the companies where I previously worked. You know, the big, fancy ones that they give their shareholders to show, well, profit and loss. Not to worry though. The lady at the bank explained that a simple statement was all that they required, and she faxed me a sample to get me started. The sample was that of a self-employed gardener. My case was different and yours will be too, but it is a general format and you fill in what you need to show your financial standing.

Even if you think that you'll never want a loan or have outside investors, you still need this form, because the IRS requires businesses, large or small, to maintain profit-and-loss statements.

Sometimes these are called earnings statements or income statements. It sounds like a big deal, but it is really just a condensed version of your expenditures and receipts records for a certain period of time. In other words, it is a running total of your incoming money on one column and your outgoing money on the other (rounded off to the nearest dollar). If you keep this up on a quarterly basis, then you'll be aware of whether or not you are actually making any money, and you will be prepared for the time when this record is required by an outside source. (See page 108.)

Sign-up sheets

Put out sign-up sheets whenever you can. I bring mine to classes with me and ask all of my students to sign up for my e-mail lists. Then I can send out notices such as when I'll be teaching in their area next or if I have things to sell on eBay or something new and exciting to pass along. When you sell at shows, sign-up sheets are the perfect way to build your mailing list. I just did a show called An Artful Journey in Jacksonville, Florida. I had my sheets out on my table—very cut and dry, very functional. When checking out all the other vendors, I noticed that Barbara McGuire's sign-up sheet was gorgeous! On a clipboard, with pen attached, the sheet had a colorful picture of her artwork across the top and it caught my attention immediately. I learned from Barbara that weekend. You can bet that my new sign-up sheets are extra-special, too. And be sure to state exactly what people are signing up for at the top of your sheet. (See page 109.)

Items Out List

Date out	Item and Qty	Name and Address	Phone	Date in and Follow-up info

Purchase Order

Your Company Name
Your mailing address
Your phone number

Date:_____

Your e-mail address and/or Web site

P.O. #_____

Vendor:

Item number	Description and color	Qty	Price	Extended price
		Total:		

Invoice

Your Company Name
Your mailing address
Your phone number

Date: _____

Your Web site and/or e-mail address

Invoice # _____

Bill to:

Ship to:

Method of Shipment:		Terms:		Page #	

Qty	Item number	Description and color	Price	Unit	Disc %	Extended

Notes:		Sub Total:	
		Sales Tax:	
		Freight:	
		Less Coupons:	
		Balance Due:	

Inventory List

Date Created	Item Number	Name & Description	Qty.	Cost to Make	Sell Price	Placement	Date Sold

Month of:							
Income				Expenses			

Income

Day	Activity	Amount
1		
2		
3		
4		
5		
6		
7		
8		
9		
10		
11		
12		
13		
14		
15		
16		
17		
18		
19		
20		
21		
22		
23		
24		
25		
26		
27		
28		
29		
30		
31		
Total up to this month		
Total this month		
Total to date		

Notes:

Expenses

Acct. No.	Deductible Accounts	Total up to this month	Total this month	Total to date
1	Materials			
2	Accounting			
3	Advertising			
4	Auto Expense			
5	Cartons, etc.			
6	Contributions			
7	Delivery			
8	Electricity			
9	Entertainment			
10	Freight			
11	Heat			
12	Insurance			
13	Interest			
14	Laundry			
15	Legal Expense			
16	Licenses			
17	Misc. Exp.			
18	Office exp.			
19	Postage			
20	Rent			
21	Repairs			
22	Tax-sales			
23	Tax-soc.sec.med			
24	Tax-State U. I.			
25	Tax-other			
26	Selling Exp.			
27	Supplies			
28	Telephone			
29	Trade Dues			
30	Traveling Exp.			
31	Wages and Comm.			
32	Water			
33				
34				
35				
	Sub-total			
	Non-Deductible			
51	Notes payable			
52	Federal Inc. Tax			
53	Loans payable			
54	Loans recd.			
55	Personal			
56	Fixed assets			
57				
		Total up to this month	Total this month	Total to date

Your Name Company
Profit-and-Loss Statement
For the quarter ended June, 20xx

Income
Gross Sales		$43,990
Bad Debt	- $325	
Discounts	- $250	
Returns	- $00	
Theft	- $178	
Interest, Royalties		$1,200
Other Income		$00
Total Gross Income		$44,437

Expenses
Cost of Goods Sold:		
Merchandise and Materials Purchased	- $17,211	
Freight	- $748	
Advertising and Promotion	- $2,535	
Interest on Loans	- $48	
Office Expenses	- $168	
Professional Fees	- $00	
Business Subscriptions	- $48	
Rent	- $1,800	
Sales Expenses (Booth Fees, Etc.)	- $500	
Shipping and Postage	- $328	
State and Local Taxes and Licenses	- $1,000	
Travel Expenses	- $2,899	
Utilities	- $395	
Total Expenses	-$27,680	

Net Income Before Taxes		$16,757
Income Tax	- $6,850	
Net Income After Taxes		$9,907

Sign-up for Sandra McCall's E-mail List

Name:	E-mail address:

Licenses, zoning and rules...oh my!

As soon as you actually make your first sale, guess who is first in line to strip you of some of that money? You got it—the Internal Revenue Service. It does not matter that you don't think of yourself as a business or that you only make a little extra money with your crafts or that you say it is just a hobby. The government wants to collect taxes on anything you earn. Period. You can have a craft business or a craft hobby, but all the money you make is extra income and must be reported on Form 1040–Schedule C. If you decide to call yours a "craft hobby" income, then you can deduct some materials but only up to the amount of your craft earnings. It actually makes more sense to call yourself a business because you can claim a lot more deductions, which extend into your other household earnings. This applies to joint filings with a spouse as well.

Most cities require the home crafter to buy a home-based business license. Again, it does not matter what you call yourself, if you make money by making items for sale in your home then you must buy a license. That's where "zoning" comes into play.

In some states, this business license also acts as your resale license. Or you may need a separate resale license to purchase materials wholesale. This is the number you reference when you pay sales tax on the items you make. The licenses are pretty inexpensive. In exchange for your application money, the state happily sends you your sales tax and revenue forms. While you are at your city hall, check to see if your city requires you to pay city taxes—some cities do.

Read on for what you need to keep your business on the up and up as far as the state and federal authorities go.

Business licenses

For your business, you need to buy a permit to operate in your city. These permits can be obtained at your local city hall. They are relatively inexpensive, ranging from $25–$40 and may cover six months or a year, depending on where you live. They will also ask for your business name and if you are the sole owner of your business or if you have a partner. If you have a partner, take her along with you. She will have to complete some papers too.

Fictitious Business Name Statement

If you choose to do business with a name other than your own, you will have to file a Fictitious Business Name Statement and take out an ad in the local paper declaring that you are who you are and that you are doing business as whatever your business name will be. So, if I name my company Super Star Sandy, then my ad would read Sandra McCall d/b/a (that means "doing business as") Super Star Sandy.

Check out the classified section of any newspaper under the "Legal Notices" heading. You'll see where several people have filed a Fictitious Business Name Statement. You can file in any newspaper in your county. So, if you do not want your neighbors, or anyone else who may read a particular paper, to know what you are up to, place the ad in a different paper. Your newspaper of choice will let you know exactly the wording you need to provide. Many even let you fill in the ad and submit it over the Internet.

Zoning ordinances

If you work out of your home, you probably have to deal with "Zoning Clearance" for your city or county. The clerk at city hall can help you with that, too. The local authorities need to know that your enterprise will not adversely affect traffic in your neighborhood. They also want to be assured that you will not cause a fire with any caustic chemicals that you may be using, and that everything you're doing is legal. They need to know that your home and your neighborhood will be safe and undisturbed by your new business.

If you plan on burning anything or using hazardous chemicals in your crafts, such as firing ceramics in an open-air pit or garbage can (as in Raku pottery), you need to contact the local fire department. You may need to get a permit. They will let you know if this is even allowable in your neighborhood when you call them. If you think this is a pain-in-the-neck step and that no one needs to know about your art anyway and then something blows up or catches fire, you may have more than just ash on your face. Don't skip this step.

If you rent, your landlord has to sign forms of permission to be filed with your city hall. They want to know that your landlord knows what you are up to in his building. This is to protect him in the event of damage or liability on his property. He may have to take out extra insurance on his homeowner's policies as well, so expect him to quiz you on your proposed home business.

Federal Trade Commission

If you make wearable art or manufacture any type of soap or cosmetics, you need to follow strict labeling guidelines as determined by the Federal Trade Commission (FTC) in the Federal Packaging and Labeling Act. I recommend looking up all this information on the Internet. Search "Federal Packaging and Labeling Act" and you will see right where to look for more information than you will probably ever need. By the way, when I thought about making artisan soaps and cosmetics, I found out that one of the stipulations is that you must not make anything that is "putrid." It made me laugh to think that the lawmakers felt the need to include that rule.

The FTC also makes rulings concerning mail-order businesses, many of which apply to any sales at conventions and over the Internet. For instance, you must ship items within thirty days or within the time specified in your advertising. If you do not meet these requirements, then the customer has the right to return such items for

Dancing with the Moon
by Les Gains
PHOTO BY LES GAINS

a full refund. There are lots of other rules that may apply to your particular activities, so be sure to read them, if for no other reason than to help you establish your own policies on your sales. You'll get a lot of ideas that you may not think of by yourself.

Resale licenses

If you need to buy supplies and materials to create your crafts, then you need a resale license. In some states, it is called a Transaction Privilege License. This allows you to buy your supplies wholesale and without paying taxes on materials at the time of purchase. Then you can use that product to create your art. When you sell it, you charge taxes and then, at the end of the year, you pay the sales tax that you would have paid when you bought the supplies.

To get a resale license or Transaction Privilege License, contact your State Department of Revenue. You can usually find the number in the phone book and apply for a license over the phone. Instructions will accompany your license when it arrives in the mail.

Keep your resale license with you so you can hand it to the shop clerk where you buy your supplies. The store needs to make a copy in order to keep a record of your business so they can show the state why they did not collect taxes from you on those sales.

Don't worry about where to find the appropriate sales tax form to submit to the state at tax time. When you get a resale license, the state goes on alert, and they eagerly and promptly send you tax forms, whether you are happy to get them or not.

Polymer Clay Pendants
by Deborah Anderson
PHOTO BY LIV AMES

Contract labor

If you perform a service with your crafts, such as teaching classes or writing books, then you're considered "contract labor." The person or company that required your services pays you and files 1099 forms. At the end of the year, they send you the 1099 forms, which you use in place of or in addition to your W-4 forms. When you go to file employment taxes, you will see where the monies from 1099 forms go on the tax forms. If you remain the only worker in your business, then your social security number will still be what you use to identify yourself with the federal government at tax time. If you have employees, you must file for an Employer Identification Number (EIN). You can find out how to do this and obtain much more information on the IRS Web site at www.irs.gov/businesses/small/article/0,,id=97872,00.html.

Business checking accounts

You may wish to open a business checking account. Don't forget to put your logo on the business checks! This is another opportunity to make an impression on all who see your checks so that people see your logo over and over. The more they see your name and logo, the more they will recognize and remember you and your business. Our government does not require you to open a business account. However, if the feds come calling, it's easier to show that you are in business if you keep your household money separate from your business money. Of course, there are costs, pros, and cons involved in each type of account. Check with your banker to see which account is best for you.

By keeping finances separate, you will be better able to see exactly where your money is going in your expenditures. If your money is combined with your husband's money and you are paying both household and business bills out of one account, it's easy for you to live in la-la land about how much money you are actually making. Your profits and losses become a blur, especially if you are like me and are inclined to avoid all thoughts of grown-up business. If you don't know whether you are succeeding or not, then you may end up in deep finan-

cial trouble before you even know it. Even if you hate the business stuff, you must force yourself to take this responsibility seriously.

Insurance

If you bring merchandise to trade shows or craft fairs, or if you have any type of business where you have tangible art for sale, then you may want to invest in more than just homeowner's or renter's insurance. Remember, you put a lot of time and effort into making these goods, and your time is one of the most valuable assets that you own. Some homeowner's insurance covers your art, but check to see if it applies if your car is broken into, if your art is stolen from a consignment gallery, or if people break your handcrafts at a craft fair. Will your insurance cover you if your stuff gets hit by a big wind and gets thrown into the vendor's stall next to you? Will it cover you when you damage someone else's art with your stall? Hey, I've seen it happen. At an outdoor craft mart, many of us witnessed an umbrella lift up and take off in a strong dust devil. It bumped into a couple booths and then landed smack in the middle of another booth. No one was hurt, thank heaven, but it sure did break a couple pots and muck up several booths. There are many insurance companies that specialize in art and craft stock. Cruise the Internet, read trade magazines and get personal testimonials so you can choose the right insurance company for your business.

You may need to up your homeowner's insurance, especially if you use a lot of specialized tools and materials. Check with your insurance agent about extra liability insurance if you plan on having buyers coming into your home on a regular basis.

If you sell facial lotion, bath salts, anything edible, anything at all that may be harmful to anyone whether real or imagined, you should cover yourself with Product Liability Insurance. Insurance companies that deal in business or commercial insurance policies can help you out with all the details on this type of insurance.

Sea and Firefly
by Roberta Altschuler
PHOTO BY ROBERTA ALTSCHULER

CHAPTER 14
Reassess the Situation

Be adventurous
By Roberta Altschuler, beader, stamp designer and founder of rubber-stamp company ERA Graphics

A problem I see all around me is artists that have found a comfortable niche and never leave it. Yes, it is scary to experiment and try new and different things. Simply showing your art makes you vulnerable to criticism and judgment. However, you must remain open to change, growing and pushing the envelope of various mediums. Otherwise, you run the risk of getting stale and the whole "enterprise" becomes "work." I have promised myself that I will stop if my beading isn't fun anymore. So far I feel that I have only scratched the surface, and when there is nowhere else to go I will stop.

Our Lady of the
Eternal Double Latté

*Our Lady of the
Eternal Double Latté*
by Michael Jacobs
PHOTO BY BILL WICKETT

A java jump start

By Michael Jacobs, sculptural-book, wood-craft and leather-craft artist

My wife Judy and I start almost every day in a coffee shop, and I always have a
couple of my handmade sketchbooks with me. I relish this time and use it to relax
and play with ideas. I rarely experience "art blockers" and just looking through my
sketchbooks gets my creative juices flowing. I also bring photographs of art, archi-
tecture, craft objects, jewelry, furniture and pottery, culled from magazines and
catalogs. I often scan the photos as I'm looking through my own sketchbooks. New
ideas pop up, or ways to combine ideas. For example, the shape of part of a con-
crete building and a free-form reed basket might be the starting point for a book
sculpture in wire and covered mat board. I'll make a quick thumbnail sketch and
then make many small sketches on the same theme, incorporating refinements
and even major changes along the way. These eventually lead to larger drawings
with notes on possible materials and construction techniques. Mostly, I work in
3-D and like to have flexibility as I go, so the drawings aren't always real tight.
Sometimes, I create a working drawing or sketch and then start the project. Other
times, I refer to the thumbnail sketches and wing it, making revisions as I construct
project models to work out design and structural challenges. This is the part of the
creative process I enjoy most of all.

The one true thing about being self-employed is that you continually need to reassess your situation—you want to take stock of your progress or lack thereof, as is sometimes the case. Basically, you need to ask yourself, "Are things going well for me? Is this what I really want to be doing at this time?"

When time is most precious, the phone keeps ringing, the printer is out of ink, and you know you're almost out of money, the pressure to be creative is almost paralyzing. Those are the times that you will seriously question your career choice and wonder if you should just go back to that forty-hour work week and let someone else call all the shots. In this case, I say, get back under the covers and ignore the world for a day. Surely, you say, she must be nuts. Time is so valuable and there is none left. There isn't one minute to waste, let alone a full day. I say that it is at these times that you must waste a day! When you feel paralyzed with fear and ineptitude then you must take a day to recoup your energies. If you do not, it will catch up with you. You will start making poor decisions and you will want to start staying in bed every day. Sometimes the most reinvigorating exercise is to do nothing—just watch the day go by. But, put a time limit on wasting away. You know that you don't really want to go back to getting up at the same time Monday through Friday for the privilege of having to get to work at the same time every day. You don't really want to have to set the alarm clock just to enjoy the same office politics every day, on and on and on. So, take a break and then get back to the work that you love.

It is never too late to change tracks.

Sometimes you have to wake up and face the fact that you need to start over. You may find that, on your chosen track, you're losing money or your mind, maybe both. There can be a couple downsides to starting over. One of them is the inevitable feeling of being a failure. Maybe you will worry about what your friends and acquaintances will think. Don't look at it that way! Hey, you're a success because you tried, because you went places that you never thought possible, and because you recognize when it is time to get out. There is no shame in starting over if you have already given it your best shot.

I have, always it seems, had a phrase sticking to the back of my head. It is something that my mom paraphrased for me a long time ago. Neither of us knows who said this first, but it is so true. "Clinging to the wreckage isn't the same thing as being rescued." Often people are afraid to let go of the wreckage and move on, but sometimes it is the only sensible thing to do.

Art blockers

The time will come when you're overworked, completely drained or under a mind-numbing deadline. How can you come up with new designs when all you feel is panic? All you really want to do is climb back under the covers and stay there until everyone has forgotten about you and everything you agreed to do. Unless you want to chuck it all, the work must go on. You've got a big show com-ing up, but you have no new ideas. What should you do? How do you handle the art blockers?

There are several avenues that will provide you with forward momentum once again. First, realize that you're not alone. Everyone has blockers at some point. Second, get out of bed and take some advice from your fellow artists. My art blocker list goes like this:

• Take a deep, calming breath and just start. Grab a sheet of paper, paint and a brush and layer color on top of color. Don't try to make "a painting," just an interesting texture. It's not a waste of time; you can use this paper as a background in some other work. For now, your goal is to concentrate on freeing your mind. Enjoy color for color's sake and texture for the beauty of texture. Remember what it's like to make art for play, not to meet deadlines. This is my number one remedy for art blockers because the mere action of putting color and brush to paper leads to ideas and ideas always generate new ideas. Soon, the ideas will flow, so keep a notebook ready!

• Pack a lunch and a sketchbook and get out of the house in search of beauty. You can find it on a walk in the park or a day hike in nature. Have you ever noticed a twig or a rock so beautiful that it inspires your jewelry? Or paintings? Maybe it's the very act of moving or the time for quiet introspection, but hiking always does it for me.

• If I don't have time for a hike, I go to some of my favorite stores or galleries. Seeing the work of others, up close and in real life, always reinvigorates me.

• Close your eyes. Darken the room, get comfortable, lie back and relax. Let your mind wander, but focus on the backs of your eyelids. What imaginary pictures do you see in all those blinking lights and patterns? Doesn't it look like sparkling jewelry or abstract paintings? Keep a notebook handy for this exercise as well.

• Dive into your books and magazines again. You'll probably run across something that jiggles a little creativity loose. I like to look into decorating magazines and pick out a room with a small painting on the walls. You know, the ones where you can tell that it's a painting, but it's too small to see clearly. I like to stare at it and imagine what the painting could be and then go paint my version of it.

• Clean the house. Again, I think being active can generate a spark in creative capabilities. Or maybe it's the action of performing a task that's been performed a million times that frees your mind for more artful imaginings. Perhaps it clears the cobwebs in more ways than one.

Burnout

Sometimes burnout is a blessing in disguise. Burnout is your inner self telling you to give it a break. In my case, I realized I needed to take a break from teaching art classes. So I did. For two years, I painted houses when I wasn't painting my own. Even though I loved it, I wasn't a very good house painter because I was afraid of heights and getting up on the ladder. But, the solitary work was good for me. I had time to think.

When you teach, the pressure is on to generate new classes that will appeal to a lot of people. I tried to please as many as I could with my proposed classes. The result was that I found myself losing focus. I was losing me. I realized that I needed time to reflect, to paint houses and canvases—to paint what I wanted to paint, not what I thought would sell. Desperate to get back to what was important to me, I quit teaching and it worked out beautifully. Now I'm back to teaching but with a whole new attitude. I already knew that I couldn't please everyone, but now I don't even attempt to please half of everyone. And I teach only classes I believe in, not whatever is asked of me just to please.

Sometimes you only require a short time-out, but other times you need to take a whole new direction. When burnout happens, pay attention!

The power of positive thinking

A person who's near and dear to me was quick to ask, "Aren't there already too many craft books out there? Does the world really need another craft book?" Even though I know her questions aren't intentionally hurtful, they cause me to doubt myself. My sister, Jenny, often comes to the rescue of my sometimes-fragile ego. One day, she brought this quote to my attention:

"Don't worry about what the world needs. Ask what makes you come alive and do that. Because what the world needs are people who have come alive."
—Howard Thurman

You can't imagine how many times I have referred to that quote. I even pull it out in classrooms when others have the same nagging doubts. Sometimes negativity, including your own, will trample your positive spirit. There will be many naysayers. Don't let them get you down! Think, *They just don't get it. That has little to do with me or my efforts.*

Yes, there are a lot of craft books on the shelves, but, lucky for us, the turnaround time is quick. We creative types are always on the lookout for new books and magazines. We want to see up-to-date publications featuring other artists. We need to stay current by keeping an eye on trends, and we want to read about things that interest us. We're a large group of consumers who look to books and magazines for inspiration and education. We also need these publications for our own writing outlets and even as advertising outlets for our names and our work. So, don't think of the massive array of books and magazines on the market as a negative thing. There's room for everyone. Thank goodness there are a lot of craft books on the market! Writing about your craft is one of the best ways to make money with your talents.

Believe
by pj dutton
PHOTO BY SANDRA McCALL

Unjunk your surroundings

By pj dutton, mixed-media artist and author

When I'm blocked, I clean my studio or go through my file drawers. I always find something I bought with a purpose in mind and it got pushed aside.

Artists' Bios

ROBERTA ALTSCHULER is a multi-media artist with an addiction to beads. She lives in Placerville, California with her husband and their pets, a white standard poodle and hundreds of very fertile koi.

Roberta started ERA Graphics, her art rubber-stamp company, more than fourteen years ago. Over the years she worked in pottery and ceramics, faux finishing, beading, calligraphy, bargello and embroidery, and silver and jewelry making. Before founding ERA Graphics, she raised a son, taught art at a junior high school, lived in Germany and Japan and dipped her toes in all seven seas.

She recalls her earliest memories that revolved around art, "When I was four, I carefully cut holes in my dress. My mother wasn't amused. I suppose my talent came from my father's mother, Lena. She was a magician with cloth. She was always knitting, crocheting and doing needlework. She was supporting an extended family with her talent and was emphatic about one thing, which she drilled into me: 'Do not do piecework.'

"Now, here I am fifty years later, and what am I doing? Piecework!"

www.eragraphics.com
Roberta@eragraphics.com

DEBORAH ANDERSON took a ceramics class in high school and was delighted to sell some of her class projects to a local shop owner. He paid her in cash and a bag of leather scraps. Deborah used the scraps and began designing and constructing small pouches and purses. She then took a sandal-making class, which led to closed shoes and boots. She made custom footwear and accessories for many clients, including Carlos Santana. Her handcraft business flourished for more than thirty years.

Deborah and her husband raised two daughters. Deborah and her younger daughter, Marah Anderson, took a polymer-clay class and both fell in love with the medium. It became their main craft. Deborah primarily makes jewelry and beads. In 1993, Deborah, along with Desiree McCrorey, started the Southbay Polymer Clay Guild of San Jose, California. Deborah and her husband now run their own hardwood-floor business and reside in San Jose, California with their pets. In addition to helping with the hardwood-floor business, Deborah also makes and sells her jewelry and leather accessories at craft shows and galleries. She contributes projects and articles to magazines and demonstrates for several art supplies manufacturers.

www.geocities.com/thousand_canes
MarahA@aol.com

TRACI BAUTISTA began making clothes, doodling, lettering and doing "artsy" things at a young age. She now combines all of these passions in her vibrant, handmade journals and paintings that are layered with rich textures of stained papers, painted and sewn fabric, "girlie glam" ink drawings and free-style lettering. Her love for art led her to leave a career in high-tech marketing to pursue her lifelong dream of starting a creative business.

Traci is creative director and owner of treiC Designs. She designs "girlie glam," an eclectic line of hand-painted papers, custom invitations and aRt! kits for bookmaking and stamping. She teaches at art retreats throughout the country and private workshops at her aRt! loft in Fremont, California, where she lives with her two little Yorkshire terriers. Her artwork has been featured in *Somerset Studio, Cloth Paper Scissors* and various books. Her book *Collage Unleashed* from North Light Books is available now.
www.treicdesigns.com
traci@treicdesigns.com

TONI CURTIS is an accomplished doll artist who spent seventeen years creating and selling original figures. Now, she's turned to handmade books and journals.

"I live in a quiet neighborhood on the bayou. As a child, I loved hand sewing and drawing. My mother taught me to sew on her sewing machine, a skill I have carried with me through my life."

She began making cloth dolls in 1998 and drawing and painting the doll's faces and drafting many of her own patterns. She's now interested in handmade journals, altered arts and rubber stamps. Toni lives in Bastrop, Louisiana with her husband. They have two grown children and four real-life dolls, their grandchildren. Toni teaches both locally and nationally.
www.heartofthegypsy.com
www.picturetrail.com/tonij
www.artisajourney.blogspot.com

RHONDA DECANDIA has always been interested in paper arts. This interest coupled with her education in marketing and business resulted in her opening a rubber-stamp store. She enjoys helping her customers understand the scope and importance of their art through a huge variety of art supplies.
www.rhondascreativecrafting.com

pj dutton describes herself as a mixed-media artist. She teaches art classes at stores and conventions across the country. pj also creates arts samples for JudiKins Rubber Stamp Company, has authored three books about rubber stamping on vellum and has contributed to several other books. Her work has been published in *The Rubber Stamper, Somerset Studio* and *RubberStampMadness* magazines. Her favorite media at the moment are copper, metal and glass.

pj lives and creates in Festus, Missouri.
PJSTAMPS@aol.com

SARAH FISHBURN is an internationally known collage artist. She's recognized for her unexpected yet elegant combinations of bright colors, words and vintage images. Her work is constantly evolving and has recently included both photos taken in Africa and images and techniques appropriated from a modern urban tradition.

Now and again, her work appears in art magazines and can be seen gracing the pages of a shelf full of books. Sarah often participates in large collaborative works and is a frequent contributor to various fund-raising events. She lives and occasionally teaches classes in northern Colorado.
www.sarahfishburn.com
sarah@sarahfishburn.com

LES GAINS is happy to make art for art's sake. With his musician/artist grandfather's guidance, he started creating art at a very young age.

Les' compass continues to point to the arts. His professional life includes working as a photographer's assistant and stylist, making spiral-bound notebooks and working as a silk-screen artist. He's also sold illustrations to the Los Angeles Times and worked as a desktop publisher for several companies.

From 1989 to 2001, Les and his wife, Sandra McCall, owned a rubber-stamp company called Gains & McCall. When the company took off, it became too much for the two of them to handle. Not willing to give up all their other activities, the company was disbanded and the images were sold to Stamp Oasis and to JudiKins.

Les now lives in northern Arizona where he writes and produces music, sculpts 3-D figures, is a printmaker and creates colorful computer art. He is rarely seen without a camera in his backpack. And, yes, Les and Sandy still have dueling art tables.
www.arthouse525.com
lesgains@arthouse525.com

CLAUDINE HELLMUTH is one of today's leading collage artists. Her work has been chosen for fine-art poster designs, featured in numerous magazines, used as book-cover artwork, published as rubber-stamps, drink coasters, journals and more.

In addition to creating her artwork full time, Claudine teaches mixed-media collage workshops in the United States and Canada. She's written two books with North Light Books, *Collage Discovery Workshop* and *Collage Discovery Workshop: Beyond the Unexpected*. She's also produced two instructional DVDs about her techniques, has been a guest on HGTV's *The Carol Duvall Show* and DIY's *Craft Lab!*

Claudine enjoys the challenge of working with a variety of materials and cutting, pasting and painting her artworks by hand.

Claudine's studio and home are in Orlando, Florida, where she lives with her husband, and their very spoiled four-legged children.
www.collageartist.com
Chellmuth@aol.com

SARAH HODSDON started selling her mixed-media collages and note cards at local juried fine art shows and in various galleries and specialty shops after retiring from the financial industry. Now a professional designer, artist and instructor, her artwork and articles have been published in a number of nationally circulated publications, including *Expression, Somerset Home, The Rubber Stamper, Creative TECHniques, Scrap & Stamp Arts, RubberStampMadness, Stamper's Sampler* and *Vamp Stamp News* in addition to a number of manufacturer's catalogs, Web site galleries and advertisements. Sarah has two distinct lines of rubber stamps licensed by Art Declassified. When she's not creating for a specific client, she's teaching.
www.stampingtoday.com

MICHAEL JACOBS has been a mixed-media artist for more than thirty years. He's used various tools and materials—from leather and wood, to wire, plastic and paper… always paper.

For eight years he owned a custom-leather and wood-working shop in California where he created briefcases, purses, hats, headboards, signs, puzzles, boxes, photo albums, diaries and custom work of all kinds. After a ten-year stint as a hairdresser, he went back to school and graduated with honors from a two-year, commercial-art program. He then opened a design studio specializing in paper engineering, pop-ups, and 3-D props and signage.

As a Artist-in-Action for King County Solid Waste from 1992 to 1995, he conducted workshops in libraries, schools and malls on creative ways to reuse paper and other solid waste materials for bookbinding, correspondence and package wrapping. During this time he also began teaching paper-craft and bookmaking workshops.
Today, Michael's art goal is to create book works that stand alone as sculptures and require the viewer to physically interact with them. "Ultimately," he says, "I would like people to rethink what books are all about." Michael's sculptural books and wood- and leather-craft objects are in private collections throughout the United States.
www.thecreativezone.com
creativezone@earthlink.net

SHERRILL KAHN has been creating award-winning drawings, paintings and fiber artwork for almost forty years. Her work can be found in many private collections throughout the world. She loves to weave, quilt, airbrush, bead, sew, knit, crochet, draw, paint and design rubber stamps. Sherrill also makes books, jewelry and dolls; paints and decorates every surface imaginable; and constantly explores new materials and new techniques. She lives by four simple words: "Have fun" and "What if?"

Sherrill taught for thirty years in the Los Angeles public schools. She has also taught for university-extension programs and given lectures along with demonstrations to numerous art groups and organizations. Since leaving the public schools, Sherrill now teaches across the country and loves to share the joy of the creative process with her students. She's been published in magazines and books related to fiber arts and rubber-stamping. She's also authored several creative craft books and is now planning a video on creative-art techniques.

Sherrill lives in southern California with her husband. They love to travel and have been in almost every state in the United States and many foreign countries. They started a rubber-stamp company four years ago called Impress Me, which focuses on ethnic cultures and Southwest art.
www.impressmenow.com
impressme@earthlink.net

SUZANNE LAMAR has developed software solutions, marketed products (to different audiences) and refined product delivery processes contributing to the financial success of many organizations.

With more than seventeen years of professional experience, she is fluent in a broad array of software applications and technology paradigms.

Suzanne lives and works in northern California where she founded PageSage, which produces craft and hobby DVDs.
www.pagesage.com
Suzanne@pagesage.com

SYLVIA LUNA/SILVER MOON came across her art pen name when a woman was paying for her art supplies. The woman said, "Sylvia Luna…what a beautiful name! It's Silver Moon!" Sylvia took it as a sign from her muse and kept it.

Sylvia enjoys working with mixed media, mostly collage but also works with fabric, beads, metals, wood and polymer clay. She teaches art classes in the Phoenix, Arizona area. Sylvia's article "101 Ways to Alter Books" was published in *ARTitude*. Since then, she continues to contribute to various alternative art zines. She has a classroom/art studio in her home where she teaches and has brought in local and national guest artists such as Doris Arndt and Brionie Vardon Williams. She also has a second studio in northern Arizona for workshops.

Sylvia has hosted several swaps and vends at national artist conventions. Sylvia has been a contributing artist and has been featured in several magazines. She lives in Gilbert, Arizona with her "art supportive" husband and her three dogs.

www.silvermoonstudios.com
www.silvermoonstudios.com/LUNAcy.html
artmedo@aol.com

SANDRA McCALL calls herself "a rubber-stamp and multimedia expert." She makes art—from designing craft projects to writing articles for rubber-stamp/paper-arts books and magazines. She also designs rubber stamps for JudiKins and Stamp Oasis. Majoring in commercial art, she quickly decided that the field was too restrictive. She was elated to discover that there were companies out there who were willing to pay for original drawings to be turned into rubber stamps.

Sandy teaches art workshops across the United States. She's currently interested in resin casting, any type of fiber arts, beading on jewelry and fabric, soft block carving, polymer clay, making dolls and art figures of all kinds and painting canvases with acrylic paint.

Sandy has had several articles and artwork featured in major publications and one DVD with PageSage called *Fabricadabra: Material Magic With Sandra McCall*. She's written four additional North Light titles: *Making Gifts With Rubber Stamps, 30-Minute Rubber Stamp Workshop, Sandra McCall's Rubber Stamped Jewelry* and *Stamping Effects in Polymer Clay with Sandra McCall*.

Sandy lives in Arizona with her husband and best friend, fellow artist, Les Gains.
www.arthouse525.com
www.sandramccall.blogspot.com
mccallss@arthouse525.com

CATHERINE MOORE is an artist self-taught through study and life experience. Catherine grew up on a little farm in south Florida. The family business was game hens and eggs, baby quail, pheasant and guinea hens. Swans and peacocks were among their family pets. Catherine believes that "creativity is not about art making—it is about seeing. Sometimes the answers we seek are there all along, but they may be so much a part of our everyday lives we don't see them." Catherine stays busy with her family and somehow squeezes in time for her decorative-paper business, rubber stamps, collage art and writings. She's been published several times in both books and magazines.
www.characterconstructions.com
PostoDelSol@aol.com

STEPHANIE OLIN and her husband show her stamps and jewelry at rubber-stamp conventions and boutiques, craft fairs, and invitational jewelry parties. Stephanie Olin Designs offers an online catalog featuring more than 800 images and sixty sterling charms (also available in 14K gold plate) and jewelry.
www.stephanieolin.com
stephi@stephanieolin.com

GLORIA PAGE had a home business making miniature grapevine wreaths. Her husband brought her a rubber stamp to make price tags for the wreaths. This began her hobby, which led to bookmarks made with a few Southwest stamps her mother bought. From bookmarks to cards, from a hobby to a business, ImpressionsArt grew exponentially. At one point Gloria was making 10,000 cards per year, shipping them to museum and gallery/gift shops around the country.

In 2000, she self-published *Holy Moly Mackeroly!*, a memoir-styled book of her art-life experiences. In January 2006, North Light Books released Gloria's second book, *Art Stamping Workshop*.
www.impressionsart.com
Gloriapage@character.net

LISA PAVELKA is a Colorado native who resides in Las Vegas, Nevada with her husband and sons, daughter and foster daughter. She began working with polymer clays in the late 1980s and nationally distributed her line of miniature Bearly There® figurines.

Lisa also demonstrates, teaches throughout the world, appears on television, writes books, columns and articles, and appears in DVDs. She has her own line of buttons and clay/crafting products through JHB International. Her work and skills are often sought out by companies such as Dremel, Fiskars and Swarovski Crystal.

Lisa has been the recipient of numerous awards for her artwork, books and products. Her work can be found in collections belonging to the White House, Julia Roberts, Siegfried & Roy, Bernie Mac, Ben Stein and Weight Watcher's founder Jean Nidetch.

Lisa loves to volunteer her time teaching both children and adults and donates her artwork to worthy causes. She believes that "Each one of us is an artist in our own right. It just means finding your canvas—be it polymer clay, cooking, gardening or something else."

www.heartinhandstudio.com
lisapavelka@cox.net

LYNNE PERRELLA is a mixed-media artist, author, designer and workshop instructor. She's published three books, *Artist's Journals & Sketchbooks*, *Alphabetica* and *Beyond Paper Dolls*. She's on the editorial advisory board of *Somerset Studio* and *Legacy* magazines and frequently contributes to various paper-arts publications and books. She leads creativity workshops throughout the United States and abroad.

www.LKPerrella.com
lkperrella@aol.com

CAROL RAMSEY lives in Phoenix, Arizona with her husband and their five dogs and ten birds. In 1996, Carol and her husband opened a rubber-stamp shop, which lead to purchasing a struggling rubber-stamp manufacturer. They now produce rubber stamps made from original drawings, maintain a Web site and run the shop. You can find Stampotique in northern Phoenix, Arizona.

www.stampotique.com

LISA RENNER is a mixed-media artist who creates artwork that is both texturally complex and integrated with an ever-changing palette of color. Her interests include paper arts, jewelry, bookmaking, art dolls and polymer clay. A self-taught artist, Lisa teaches polymer-clay and mixed-media, paper-arts classes nationally. Her work has been published in *Belle Armoire*, *Legacy*, *Stamper's Sampler* and *Somerset Studio* magazines.

Lisa's work can also be seen in many books including *Stamp Art* by Sharilynn Miller, *The Art of Paper Collage* by Susan Pickering Rothamel, *The Complete Guide to Altered Imagery* by Karen Michel, *Alphabetica* and *Beyond the Paper Doll*, both by Lynne Perrella.

Her handmade cigar-box purses have been sold in boutiques and museum shops across the country, including the Los Angeles County Museum of Art in Los Angeles, California and The Jewish Museum in New York.

Lisa lives just north of Dallas with her husband, two children, her dog, and three very spoiled cats.

lisarenner@comcast.net

LESLEY RILEY is best known for her "Fragment" series of small fabric collages. Lesley is also an internationally known quilter and mixed-media artist with a passion for color and the written word. Her work takes the form of art quilts, fabric books, dolls and more. She has taught extensively in the United States, as well as in Australia and Italy. Her art and articles, which focus on the inspiration and creativity of women, have appeared in numerous publications and juried shows. She's the arts editor of *Cloth Paper Scissors* magazine. She's published two books, *Quilted Memories* and *Fabric Memory Books*. Lesley aspires to inspire others to find their own voice and share in the magic that is art. When she's not teaching, writing or making art, Lesley loves spending time with her husband, six children and four (so far) grandchildren.

www.LaLasLand.com
www.myartheart.blogspot.com
Lrileyart@aol.com

OLIVIA THOMAS has earned a living as a tailor, running her own shop. Her love soon turned toward making primitive cloth dolls. She has established herself as a leading expert in folk-art doll design and construction. A mixed-media artist, teacher, doll maker and textile guru, Olivia is now the proud owner of a successful wholesale business called Olive Rose. You can find her dolls in galleries across the United States.

Olivia's stamps have been published in a majority of the rubber-stamp and scrapbooking magazines, including *Somerset Studio* and *Legacy*. Her dolls and fabric work have been featured in the *Art Doll Quarterly* and *Quilting Arts* magazines and in Sharilynn Miller's book, *The Stamp Artist's Project Book*. Olivia teaches at stamp shops, art retreats and conventions.

www.oliverose.com
pezman@concentric.com

JUDI WATANABE has always loved to draw and doodle. She thinks that an important aspect of her rubber-stamp business is "teaching customers how to use them. Very few people instinctively pick up a stamp and see the potential for great art." Judi holds a Bachelor of Science degree in recreation and leisure studies. Judi and her husband live and work in southern California.

www.judikins.com

Resource Guide

Federal agencies
Department of Commerce
www.doc.gov
Federal Trade Commission
www.ftc.gov
Food and Drug Administration
www.fda.gov
Internal Revenue Service
www.irs.gov
Small Business Administration
www.sba.gov
Library of Congress
Copyright Information Kit #115,
(202) 707-9100
United States Copyright Office
www.loc.gov/copyright
United States Patent and Trademark Office
www.uspto.gov

Trade associations
CHA (Craft & Hobby Association)
319 East 54th Street
Elmwood Park, NJ 07407
(201) 794-1133
www.hobby.org

Guilds and organizations
American Craft Council
72 Spring Street
New York, NY 10012
www.craftcouncil.org
(800) 724-0859
National Association of Independent Artists (NAIA)
www.naia-artists.org
Volunteer Lawyers for the Arts
The Paley Building
1 East 53rd Street, 6th Floor
New York, NY 10022
(212) 319-ARTS (2787) ext. 1
www.vlany.org

Online Information
www.craftmarketer.com
Warm Snow Publishers
Craftmarketer.com
P.O. Box 75
Torreon, NM 87061
(505) 384-1195
www.writersmarket.com
(800) 317-6758

Books
Crafting as a Business (Sterling)
by Wendy Rosen
Guerrilla Marketing: Secrets for Making Big Profits From Your Small Business (Houghton Mifflin)
by Jay Conrad Levinson
Handmade for Profit! Hundreds of Secrets to Success in Selling Arts and Crafts
(M. Evans and Company)
by Barbara Brabec
Homemade Money: Starting Smart! How to Turn Your Talents, Experience, and Know-How into a Profitable Homebased Business That's Perfect for You! (M. Evans and Company)
by Barbara Brabec
Small Time Operator, 10th Edition: How to Start Your Own Business, Keep Your Books, Pay Your Taxes & Stay Out of Trouble (Bell Springs Publishing)
by Bernard Kamoroff, CPA
Taking the Leap: Building a Career as a Visual Artist (Chronicle Books)
by Cay Lang
The Art Show Artist's Survival Guide
by the National Association of International Artists
www.naia-artists.org
The Complete Idiot's Guide to Getting Published (Alpha)
by Sheree Bykofsky and Jennifer Basye Sander
Writer's Market (F+W Publications)
by Robert Brewer

Magazines
American Craft Magazine
72 Spring Street
New York, NY 10012
(800) 724-0859
www.craftcouncil.org
Art Calendar
Art Calendar
1500 Park Center Drive
Orlando, FL 32835
(877) 415-3955
www.artcalendar.com

The Artist's Magazine
The Artist's Magazine
4700 E. Galbraith Road
Cincinnati, OH 45236
(800) 333-0444
www.artistsmagazine.com

The Crafts Report
The Crafts Report
P.O. Box 1992
Wilmington, DE 19899
(800) 777-7098
www.craftsreport.com

Entrepreneur Magazine
Entrepreneur Media Inc.
2445 McCabe Way, Ste. 400
Irvine, CA 92614
(800) 274-6229
www.entrepreneur.com

Sunshine Artist
Palm House Publishing
4075 L.B. McLeod Road, Suite E
Orlando, FL 32811
(800) 597-2573
www.sunshineartist.com

Services
PayPal
www.paypal.com
(Online payment, collections,
and credit card processing)

Etsy
www.etsy.com
(Online marketplace for your arts and crafts)

Materials
Arizona Art Supply
118 W. Indian School Road
Phoenix, AZ 85013
(602) 264-9514

Papers and supplies
Karen Foster Design, Inc
623 North 1250 West
Centerville, UT 84014
(801) 451-9779
www.karenfosterdesigns.com

Rubber-stamp companies
Clearsnap, Inc.
P.O. Box 98
Anacortes, WA 98221
(888) 448-4862
www.clearsnap.com

ERA Graphics
1705 Big Oak Road
Placerville, CA 95667
(530) 344-9322
www.eragraphics.com

Hero Arts Rubber Stamps, Inc.
1343 Powell Street
Emeryville, CA 94608
www.heroarts.com

Impress Me Rubber Stamps
17116 Escalon Drive
Encino, CA 91436
(818) 788-6730
www.impressmenow.com

JudiKins
17803 S. Harvard Blvd.
Gardena, CA 90248
(310) 515-1115
www.judikins.com

Karen Foster Design, Inc
623 North 1250 West
Centerville, UT 84014
(801) 451-9779
www.karenfosterdesigns.com

Stampotique Originals
www.stampotique.com
Stephanie Olin Designs
6171 Foxshield Dr.
Huntington Beach, CA 92647
(714) 848-1227
www.stephanieolin.com

Loose Ends
2065 Madrona Ave. SE
Salem, OR 97302
(866) 390-7457
www.looseends.com

Papers by Catherine
P.O. Box 306
Yorktown Heights, NY 10598
(914) 245-7706
www.paperaddict.com

Plaid Enterprises
(800) 842-4197
www.plaidonline.com

Index

Indulge your creative side with these inspiring titles from North Light Books!

LIVING THE CREATIVE LIFE
Ricë Freeman-Zachery

Living the Creative Life answers your questions about creativity: What is creativity anyway? Where do ideas come from? How do successful artists get started? How do you know when a piece is finished? Author Ricë Freeman-Zachery has compiled answers to these questions and more from 15 successful artists in a variety of mediums—from assemblage to fiber arts, beading to mixed-media collage. This in-depth guide to creativity is full of ideas and insights from inspiring artists, shedding light on what it takes to make art that you want to share with the world, and simply live a creative life.

ISBN-10: 1-58180-994-8, ISBN-13: 978-1-58180-994-7
paperback with flaps, 144 pages, Z0949

KALEIDOSCOPE
Suzanne Simanaitis

Kaleidoscope delivers your creative muse directly to your workspace. Featuring interactive and energizing creativity prompts ranging from inspiring stories to personality tests, doodle exercises, purses in duct tape and a cut-and-fold shrine, this is one-stop-shopping for getting your creative juices flowing. The book showcases eye candy artwork and projects with instruction from some of today's hottest collage, mixed-media and altered artists.

ISBN-10: 1-58180-879-8, ISBN-13: 978-1-58180-879-7
paperback, 144 pages, Z0346

EXPRESSIONS
Donna Smylie and Allison Tyler Jones

Whether you're a scrapbooker, amateur photographer, papercrafter or memory artist, this behind-the-camera guide shows you how to snap extraordinary photos of ordinary life. Authors Donna Smylie and Allison Tyler, co-founders of 7 Gypsies, show you inspiring ways to inject meaning and emotion into your portrait photos. Each chapter includes a sampling of stunning photo display projects to inspire you to creatively showcase your images.

ISBN-10: 1-58180-909-3, ISBN-13: 978-1-58180-909-1
paperback, 128 pages, Z0526

ARTIST TRADING CARD WORKSHOP
Bernie Berlin

Find instruction and ideas for using a variety of mediums and techniques to make artist trading cards to collect and swap. Whatever your crafting background, you'll find innovative artistic techniques for making cards, including collage, painting, metal working, stamping and more. These gorgeous miniature works of art are a great way to introduce yourself to a new medium—and to make friends along the way. The book even offers suggestions for starting your own artistic community to trade techniques and cards.

ISBN-10: 1-58180-848-8, ISBN-13: 978-1-58180-848-3
paperback, 128 pages, Z0524

These books and other fine North Light books are available at your local craft retailer or bookstore or online suppliers.